The Family Vegetarian

Mary Norwak

MEREHURST

LONDON

Published 1992 by Merehurst Limited
Ferry House, 51/57 Lacy Road, Putney
London SW15 1PR

By arrangement with WI Books Ltd,
in association with Southgate Publishers Ltd,
Glebe House, Church Street, Crediton, Devon EX17 2AF

First published 1991

Copyright © 1991 WI Books Ltd

ISBN 1-85391-326-X

A catalogue record for this book is available from the British Library.

Printed in Great Britain by Short Run Press Ltd, Exeter

CONTENTS

INTRODUCTION

Many individuals and families have traditionally followed a vegetarian diet, but in recent years a large new group of 'vegetarians' has chosen a different way of eating. These are the non-meat eaters, particularly evident in the female population under the age of twenty-five. This way of life has been adopted for a variety of reasons. Young children, for instance, often do not like the appearance, texture and flavour of red meat, while older people also begin to reject it for digestive reasons, even after a long lifetime as carnivores. Small children grow into schoolchildren, much influenced by their friends and the attention drawn by the media to factory farming and alleged cruelty. Students become even more intense about non-meat eating on these grounds. They also feel they cannot afford this ingredient in their meals, and that land would be better devoted to growing crops for humans rather than for animals who are then killed to provide our food.

Whatever the reasons for eliminating red meat from the diet, many people will still eat white meat in the form of poultry, or game which they consider 'free range'. Others will not eat meat in any form but are happy to include fish in their meals. Eggs and cheese are acceptable to those who are not vegan, which involves eliminating all dairy produce too.

With the exception of vegans, who need a very carefully planned and balanced diet, all other types of non-meat eaters can easily be included in family meals without being made to feel different or being accused of causing extra work at meal preparation time. Often they are treated badly at home and in public eating places, being expected to eat just a plate of vegetables without the family's meat, or to make do with a cheese salad or plain omelette in a restaurant.

The aim of this book is to provide a variety of delicious non-meat dishes which can be enjoyed by the whole family without being aggressively 'worthy'. They are just as suitable for the full-blown vegetarian as for some one who simply does not want to eat a piece of meat. The dishes may be enjoyed just as they are, while some members of the family will use them with their traditional roasts or grills. These dishes will not tax the cook who is already working hard to provide for the majority of the family, but will simply be an extension of the usual repertoire.

Luckily ethnic dishes are now very popular, and many of these are ideal for the purpose of this book, for they evolved among people who could rarely afford meat and who had to make the best of cheap ingredients cooked in very simple ways. We are also helped now by the growth in non-animal products in health food stores and supermarkets. A huge range of grains, beans and pulses are available, with a much wider choice of vegetables, and many special vegetarian substitutes for fat and cheeses, traditional sauces and dressings. In this book, recipes have been developed using vegetable fats and vegetable stock, but some of the new non-meat eaters will not worry unduly at the use of butter, rennet-based cheese, gelatine and chicken stock cubes, if the vegetarian substitutes are not available.

As with all good cooking, the aim is to produce light, colourful food with a pleasant texture, far removed from the heavy brown solidity of some traditional vegetarian dishes. The most important thing for the cook to remember is to look and taste frequently, so that the best use is made of fresh herbs, fruit juices, flavoured vinegars and oils, spices, sea salt and freshly ground pepper, and it is important that the finished dishes are presented attractively so that the whole family wants to try them.

BASIC NUTRITION

A well-balanced diet is essential for the old and young, male and female, not only to aid growth but but also to maintain the body and its functions throughout life. Food fads come and go, while the slimming diet is always with us, but certain basic nutrition facts do not change and must be understood if the body is to remain fit, healthy and good-looking.

Carbohydrates

Energy is provided by carbohydrates, fats and proteins, but proteins also aid the growth and maintenance of body tissue. It is very important that adequate carbohydrates are eaten to give energy, to help break down fat stores, and to allow proteins to get on with their work of body building and maintenance rather than energy. *Starch carbohydrates* from cereals, rice and pulses also contain protein and minerals, and are therefore less fattening than *sugar carbohydrates.* Sugar carbohydrates provide quick energy from sugar, honey and dried fruit but if over-used and not burned-off will fatten without nourishing. *Cellulose* is a carbohydrate which cannot be digested by the human body, but it adds valuable bulk and aids bowel movement. It is provided by wholegrain cereals, bran, nuts, and the cell walls of fruit and vegetables.

Proteins

Protein is essential for the growth and maintenance, necesssary for the development or replacement of bones, muscles, skin and blood.

Proteins consist of *amino acids,* eight of which are essential for adults, and ten for growing children. Protein from animal sources usually contains all these essential amino acids, while vegetable proteins, with the exception of soya, do not contain all of them. Lack of protein will result in retarded growth and development and increased susceptibility to disease. Vegetable proteins are derived from cereals, pulses, nuts and bread; if a mixture of these is eaten at the same meal, there will be an adequate intake of all the essential amino acids.

Fats

Fats provide energy for warmth and work, but can also make body fat if used in excess. They are however essential to the diet as they supply fat-soluble vitamins A, D and E, and low fat intake will result in reduced energy, poor skin, lacklustre hair, poor teeth and bones, and poor eyesight. Fat provides twice as much energy as carbohydrates, so intake should certainly be controlled. It is preferable to use polyunsaturated fats and oils to reduce the incidence of a build-up of cholesterol, which means a diet should not include too much butter, cream, full fat milk, cheese and egg yolks which are high in saturated fatty acids.

Minerals

Calcium is necessary for bones and teeth and for the functioning of the muscles and blood. Milk and cheese, and bread provide sufficient quantities.

Iron is essential for the functioning of the blood, and lack of it causes fatigue and anaemia. Iron is provided by eggs, green vegetables, dried fruit, cocoa powder and chocolate.

Iodine in tiny quantities helps the functioning of the thyroid gland which controls the rate at which chemical changes take place in the body. It is found in watercress and in iodized salt, and in saltwater fish if this is included in the diet.

Sodium is salt which is essential for maintaining the balance of body fluids, and lack of it will result in muscular cramps. It is taken as salt, or as the seasoning in bread, cheese, fats and many prepared foods.

Zinc is important to maintain thick hair and moist skin, and lack of it causes pre-menstrual tension, and impairs the sense of taste. It is found in eggs, nuts and seeds.

Vitamins

Vitamins are only present in very small amounts in food, but they are absolutely essential as they help the body to use the other nutrients and protect it from illness. Under medical supervision, supplementary vitamins may be taken, particularly Vitamins A and D. Excess vitamins may be stored in the body and cause illness.

Vitamin A is found in butter, margarine, cheese, eggs, almonds and peanuts and cannot be stored in the body, so a daily intake is essential. Lack of this vitamin will result in problems with eyes and eyesight, respiration, skin, and retarded growth.

Vitamin B Group cannot be stored in the body as they are water-soluble, but they are essential to the working of the body, as they help to obtain energy from food. They are found in yeast extract and brewer's yeast, wholewheat bread, cereals, pulses and cheese.

Vitamin C is essential, particularly for the growth and repair of tissues, and to increase the resistance to infection. It cannot be stored in the body and must be taken daily, and is destroyed by cutting food and by cooking. Vitamin C helps with the absorption of iron, and is found in fresh fruit and vegetables, especially citrus fruit, blackcurrants, rosehips, green vegetables, tomatoes, parsley and lettuce.

Vitamin D is very important for the absorption and laying down of calcium in the bones, it can be stored in the body. It is found in eggs, butter, margarine, milk and cod liver oil.

PLANNING MEALS

When planning meals for those who are omitting meat, and possibly fish, it is important to consider the whole day's diet to see that all nutrients are combined in suitable quantities. A combination of carbohydrates and proteins, for instance, is necessary, so that the carbohydrate provides energy and the protein builds and repairs tissue. At breakfast, this can be achieved by serving cereals with milk, or brown bread with a boiled egg. Vitamin B in the form of yeast extract or cheese or wholewheat bread helps the metabolic process and should be taken daily. Vitamin C in the form of orange juice can complete breakfast and assists the absorption of iron. Vitamin D aids the absorption of calcium from milk and bread, and this is included in the egg and in spreads such as butter and margarine. With a little practice, it is not difficult to provide well balanced nutritious meals, but the essentials of nutritional content and combination must never be forgotten.

GLOSSARY

BARLEY
Nutritious grain mainly used for soups and casseroles. *Pot barley* retains the outer husk, while *pearl barley* is smooth and polished, and more easily available. *Barley flakes* may be used for puddings. *Barley flour* is low in gluten-forming proteins and is not suitable for yeasted breads.

BEANS
Aduki (Adzuki) small, hard, round red beans with nutty flavour.

Black-eyed white beans with black 'eye', savoury flavour and soft fleshy texture when cooked.

Black similar in size and texture to red kidney beans, with shiny black skins.

Borlotti brownish-pink mottled kidney beans with full sweet flavour.

Broad usually eaten fresh, but may be dried, when they need long slow cooking.

Butter large flat white beans with soft texture and creamy flavour.

Canellini (Canneloni) may be used instead of red kidney beans and are pinkish-beige in colour.

Flageolet type of haricot bean which is young and tender when dried, with pale green colour and delicate sweet flavour.

Ful Medames (Egyptian Brown) small brown beans with smooth skins.

Haricot (Navy) small oval grey-white beans, traditionally used for 'baked beans'.

Lima similar to butter beans, but smaller and sweeter.
Mung very small green beans, mainly used to produce bean sprouts.

Pinto speckled haricot beans which turn pink when cooked.

Red Kidney (Chilli) dark red kidney beans which must be boiled hard for 10 minutes at the beginning of cooking to eliminate toxic elements, before simmering until tender.

Soya very nutritious as they provide complete protein. They are bland in flavour and take a long time to cook (see also under *soya*).

GRAINS
Bulgur (Bulgar, Burghul) Cracked wheat kernels which have been hulled, steamed and roasted. Sometimes sprinkled on bread to give a crunchy surface. Needs little cooking, and is often just soaked and softened to use as a side-dish.

Couscous Fine semolina grains coated with flour. Usually steamed and flavoured to accompany pieces of cooked vegetable, dried fruit or pieces of meat and poultry for a dish of the same name.

Maize (Sweetcorn) Cobs may be steamed and eaten, while the kernels may be used as a vegetable or an ingredient of soups and stews. Ground maize produces *cornmeal* or *polenta* used for thickening, for puddings and soft breads.

Muesli Mixture of grains with nuts and dried fruit which makes a complete and nourishing meal with milk or yogurt and fresh fruit.

Oats Useful grain which grows in a cold climate. The groat or whole grain takes a long time to cook and is rarely used. Rolled oats (porridge oats) are flaked oats used in porridge, muesli, and for baking. Oatmeal is ground oats which may be coarse, medium or fine, and may be used for porridge and for baking.

OILS

Vegetable oils such as soybean, sunflower and cotton seed oil are high in polyunsaturated fatty acids and help to lower the blood cholesterol level. They may be used for frying and for dressings, and have a bland flavour.

Olive oil is richer and more expensive than the other vegetable oils, but it has a delicious flavour for frying and dressings. It may be mixed with a light bland oil for economy and a less distinctive flavour.

Groundnut oil is made from peanuts and has a slightly nutty flavour, and gives a light crispness to dried foods.

Nut oils made from walnuts, hazelnuts or almonds are expensive but have wonderfully distinctive flavours. They should be used in small quantities for salad dressings, perhaps paired with appropriate nuts for crunchiness, and may be mixed with a bland oil for economy and a lighter flavour.

PASTA

Paste made from durum or hard wheat processed to make fine semolina which is mixed with water or egg before shaping and drying. Fresh pasta only takes about 5 minutes to cook, but packaged hard pasta needs 15-20 minutes depending on size and shape.

PULSES

Leguminous vegetables which may be dried (see also *beans*).

Chick Peas (Garbanzos) hard round peas looking like dried hazelnuts which are high in protein, with an earthy flavour.

Whole (Marrowfat Peas) dull green wrinkled peas with floury texture when cooked, excellent for soups and purées.

Split Peas inner part of peas which are split in half, and may be green or yellow. They soften quickly and are excellent for soups.

LENTILS

Similar to split peas in appearance, these are whole or split.

Red lentils are bright orange but turn yellow when cooked, with a savoury flavour.

Green lentils are dull green with a fresh spicy flavour.

Brown lentils are dark dull brown with a rich flavour.

RICE

Arborio (Italian or Risotto) short grain rice with fat grains which absorb liquid and give a creamy texture to risotto. The Arborio variety of risotto rice has a particularly fine flavour.

Basmati (Pilau) high quality long grain rice with good flavour, which does not stick when cooked.

Brown unpolished long grain rice with thin brown grains, a chewy texture and nutty flavour. Highly nutritious but takes twice as long to cook as other rices.
Carolina (Pudding) round short grains with chalky surface which become sticky when cooked. Usually best for sweet puddings, but may be used for risotto.

Patna thin long grains which become light, fluffy and separate when cooked, and used for savoury dishes, and as an accompaniment to curries.

Rice Flakes large white flakes which cook quickly for sweet soft-textured milk puddings.

SEMOLINA
Meal ground from the starchy part of the wheat grain, which may be coarse, medium or fine. Used for puddings, for thickening and for baking, and for making pasta.

SOYA
Beans which may be processed into a flour and into meat substitutes. Soya has a bland flavour which may be altered according to taste (it is often used as an almond substitute in baking), and is a complete protein food. Also made into soya milk for those who do not eat dairy produce.

TAHINI
Paste made from sesame seeds, used to flavour a variety of foods.

TOFU
Made from thickened curds of soya beans, and with a bland, subtle flavour which may be used in savoury and sweet dishes. Tofu may be plain or smoked, and is sold in blocks as 'firm', 'extra firm' and 'soft'. The product is often described as 'silken' and may be used to make dips and spreads, or used as a thickening agent instead of eggs in flans and cheesecakes. Tofu is high in protein and low in fat, and low in calories.

VEGETABLE MARGARINE
This may be used for cooking and for spreading. It contains a high proportion of polyunsaturated fatty acids. Vegetable fats provide as many calories as animal fats, and should be cut down if calorie intake has to be restricted.

VEGETARIAN SOCIETY
For general information, recipes and details of cookery courses, send s.a.e. to: The Vegetarian Society, Parkdale, Dunham Road, Altrincham, Cheshire WA14 4QG (tel: 061 928 0793).

SOUPS AND STARTERS

The first course of a meal is intended to stimulate appetite, not to satisfy it completely, so that the best dishes are not too large and not too rich. Many ethnic dishes are very suitable as appetizers, because a selection of small tempting offerings are traditionally served in hot countries to accompany drinks and to stimulate conversation in good company, and vegetables and pulses are cheap and easy to prepare in this way. Those who enjoy these tempting morsels may find them very satisfying for light lunches or suppers if eaten in larger quantities. Soup in particular makes a splendid meal when served with plenty of crusty bread, with perhaps some cheese, and fruit to follow.

VEGETABLE STOCK

MAKES 2.4 LITRES (4 PINTS)
1.25 kg (3 lb) mixed root vegetables
1 bay leaf
sprig of thyme
sprig of parsley
4 peppercorns
salt
15 g (¹/₂ oz) vegetable margarine
3.5 litres (6 pints) water

Preparation time: 15 minutes
Cooking time: 3 hours

Choose a good mixture of vegetables such as carrots, turnips, celery, onions and leeks, and make sure that they are well balanced so that there is not an over-strong flavour of any single vegetable. Do not use potatoes or green vegetables, peas or beans, which will sour the stock.

Peel the vegetables and chop them roughly. Melt the margarine and cook the vegetables over low heat, stirring well until soft but not browned. Add the herbs, peppercorns and salt and cover with water. Bring to the boil, skim, cover and simmer over low heat for 3 hours.

Leave until cool and strain through a fine sieve. Leave in a cold place. Skim off any fat before serving. The initial cooking gives a greater depth of flavour to the stock.

COURGETTE SOUP

SERVES 4–6
675 g (1 ¹/₂ lb) courgettes
50 g (2 oz) vegetable margarine
50 g (2 oz) onion
1.8 litres (3 pints) vegetable stock or water
2 eggs
3 tablespoons grated Parmesan cheese
2 tablespoons chopped fresh basil or parsley
salt and pepper

Preparation time: 10 minutes
Cooking time: 35 minutes

Do not peel the courgettes, but wash and dry them. Slice very thinly. Melt the margarine in a large thick-based pan and cook the finely chopped onion for 5 minutes over low heat until just soft but not coloured. Add the courgette slices and cook for 5 minutes, stirring often, until the courgettes are pale gold. Add the stock or water, bring to the boil, cover and simmer for 20 minutes.

Put through a sieve or blend in an electric blender or food processor, and return to a clean saucepan. Just before serving, bring to the boil. Put the eggs, grated cheese and herbs into the bottom of a large tureen or jug and season well with salt and pepper. Whisk together with a wire whisk until well mixed. Slowly pour on the boiling soup, whisking all the time. Serve at once, with additional grated Parmesan cheese if liked.

This is an excellent way of using this prolific vegetable, and the soup is full of flavour. It may be gently reheated the following day if necessary, but must not be allowed to boil.

FRESH TOMATO SOUP WITH CHEESE

SERVES 6
900 g (2 lb) ripe tomatoes
25 g (1 oz) vegetable margarine
175 g (6 oz) onions
25 g (1 oz) plain flour
1 garlic clove
sprig of parsley

sprig of thyme
1 bay leaf
600 ml (1 pint) vegetable stock or water
salt and pepper
150 ml (¹/₄ pint) double cream
1 egg yolk
100 g (4 oz) Gruyere cheese

Preparation time: 15 minutes
Cooking time: 45 minutes

Skin the tomatoes and discard the seeds. Chop the flesh roughly and keep on one side. Melt the margarine in a large pan. Chop the onions finely and add to the pan. Cook over low heat, stirring occasionally, for 10 minutes until they are soft and golden. Stir in the flour and cook for 1 minute. Add the tomatoes, crushed garlic, herbs and stock or water and season well with salt and pepper. Bring to the boil, cover and simmer for 30 minutes.

Cool slightly and blend in an electric blender or food processor, or put through a sieve. Lightly beat together the cream and egg yolk in a bowl. Add 3 tablespoons tomato mixture and mix well. Stir into pan and heat very gently. Grate the cheese. Remove soup from heat and stir in the cheese. For a thin soup, egg yolk and cream may be omitted.

SAILOR'S SOUP

SERVES 4
175 g (6 oz) dried haricot beans
2 medium carrots
1 celery stick
225 g (8 oz) canned tomatoes
2 tablespoons tomato paste
50 g (2 oz) onion
3 garlic cloves
2 tablespoons chopped fresh parsley
4 tablespoons olive oil
1 teaspoon lemon juice
salt and pepper

Garnish:
toasted or fried bread cubes

Preparation time: 10 minutes
Soaking and cooking time: overnight and 2 hours
Standing time: 1 hour

Put the beans into a bowl and cover with cold water. Leave to soak overnight. Drain well and cover with fresh cold water. Bring to the boil and cook gently for 30 minutes. Chop the carrots and celery and add to the pan. Sieve the tomatoes and add the pulp to the pan. Simmer for 5 minutes. Chop the onion finely and crush the garlic. Add to the pan with the parsley, oil, lemon juice, salt and pepper. Cover and simmer for 1 hour, adding a little water if necessary. Remove from heat and leave to stand for 1 hour. Reheat to boiling point and serve at once garnished with bread cubes

CHILLED CUCUMBER SOUP

SERVES 4
1 tablespoon oil
15 g (1 oz) onion
^{1}/$_2$ cucumber
450 ml (^{3}/$_4$ pint) natural yogurt
300 ml (^{1}/$_2$ pint) vegetable stock
1 lemon
2 tablespoons chopped fresh mint
salt and pepper

Garnish:
fresh mint leaves

Preparation time: 15 minutes

Heat the oil in a pan and add the finely chopped onion. Cook gently over low heat for 3 minutes. Peel the cucumber and cut into 5 mm (^{1}/$_4$ inch) cubes. Add to the pan and continue cooking for 5 minutes. Turn into a bowl and leave until cool.

Stir in the yogurt and stock. Grate the lemon rind and squeeze out the juice. Add the lemon rind and juice to the mixture. Stir in the chopped mint and season well with salt and pepper. Pour into 4 serving bowls and chill for 1 hour. Just before serving, garnish with mint leaves.

EGG AND OLIVE PATE

SERVES 8
15 pimento-stuffed olives
25 g (1 oz) vegetable margarine
25 g (1 oz) onion
2 garlic cloves
25 g (1 oz) plain flour
300 ml (^{1}/$_2$ pint) milk
3 eggs
75 g (3 oz) fine white or brown breadcrumbs
3 hard-boiled eggs

50 g (2 oz) capers
1 teaspoon mushroom ketchup
salt and pepper

Preparation time: 15 minutes
Cooking time: 1 hour
Preheat the oven to 180°C/350°F/Gas mark 4.

Lightly oil a 900 g (2 lb) loaf tin and line the base with greaseproof paper. Take 8 olives and slice then across in 4 slices. Arrange them on the base of the tin. Chop the remaining olives roughly and keep on one side.

Melt the margarine and add finely chopped onion and crushed garlic. Cook over low heat for 5 minutes and stir in the flour. Add the milk gradually and stir over low heat until thickened. Remove from the heat and cool for 5 minutes. Beat the eggs and stir into the sauce with the breadcrumbs. Chop the hard-boiled eggs and stir into the mixture with the reserved olives, capers and ketchup, and season well with salt and pepper. Spoon into the tin and bake for 1 hour. Leave until cold and turn on to a serving plate. Serve with salad.

BUTTER BEAN PATE

SERVES 6
225 g (8 oz) butter beans
4 tablespoons olive oil
4 tablespoons lemon juice
2 garlic cloves
2 tablespoons chopped fresh coriander
salt and pepper

Garnish:
lemon wedges
black olives

Preparation time: 10 minutes
Soaking and cooking time: overnight and 2 hours

Put the beans into a bowl and cover with cold water. Leave to soak overnight. Drain very well and cover with fresh cold water. Bring to the boil and simmer for about 2 hours until the beans are very soft. Drain very thoroughly and put into an electric blender or food processor with the oil, lemon juice, garlic and coriander. Blend to a smooth paste and then season well with salt and pepper. Turn into a serving bowl and chill before serving with a garnish of lemon wedges and olives. Serve with crisp toast.

AUBERGINE PATE

SERVES 4
2 large aubergines
1 garlic clove
2 tablespoons olive oil
2 teaspoons lemon juice
salt and pepper
2 tablespoons chopped fresh parsley

Garnish:
lemon wedges

Preparation time: 10 minutes
Cooking time: 35–40 minutes
Preheat the oven to 190°C/375°F/Gas mark 5.

Cut the aubergines in half lengthwise and place cut-side down on a greased baking sheet. Prick the skins all over with a fork. Bake for 35–40 minutes until soft. Cool to lukewarm and peel the aubergines. Put the pulp into an electric blender or food processor with the garlic clove, and blend on low speed, adding the oil a little at a time. Add the lemon juice and plenty of salt and pepper, and blend until smooth. Stir in the parsley and spoon into a serving dish. Garnish with lemon wedges and chill before serving. Serve with wholemeal bread or toast.

HUMMOUS

SERVES 4–6
100 g (4 oz) chick peas
salt and pepper
2 tablespoons tahini
2 garlic cloves
juice of 1/2 lemon
2 tablespoons olive oil
2 teaspoons chopped fresh mint

Preparation time: 10 minutes
Soaking and cooking times: overnight and 2 hours

Put the chick peas into a bowl and cover with cold water. Leave to soak overnight. Drain very well and put into a saucepan. Cover with fresh cold water, bring to the boil and then simmer gently for about 2 hours until soft. Drain well, and reserve 100 ml (4 fluid oz) cooking liquid.

Put the chick peas into an electric blender or food processor with the reserved liquid, salt and pepper tahini, garlic, lemon juice and oil. Blend until smooth and creamy. Add a little more salt and pepper if necessary. Place in a serving bowl and sprinkle with mint. Serve with crusty bread.

GUACAMOLE AND CRUDITES

SERVES 4–6
2 ripe avocados
juice of ¹/₂ lemon
2 tomatoes
25 g (1 oz) onion
1 garlic clove
¹/₂ teaspoon Worcestershire sauce
4 tablespoons natural yogurt
salt and pepper

Crudités:
4 carrots
4 celery sticks
1 green pepper
1 red pepper
¹/₂ cucumber
¹/₂ small cauliflower

Preparation time: 15 minutes
Chilling time: 1 hour

Prepare the crudités first. Take a large bowl and put in cold water and some ice cubes, and add 1 tablespoon salt. Cut the carrots, celery, red and green peppers and cucumber into matchstick pieces. Break the cauliflower into florets. Put the vegetables into salted water and leave for 1 hour. Take a serving bowl and place in the centre of a large serving dish. Drain the vegetables thoroughly and arrange neatly around the serving bowl.

Cut the avocados in half and discard the stones. Put the flesh into a bowl and mash with the lemon juice. Skin the tomatoes and discard seeds. Chop the flesh finely and add to the bowl. Grate the onion and crush the garlic and add to the bowl with the Worcestershire sauce, yogurt and plenty of salt and pepper. Beat hard until smooth. Turn into the serving dish surrounded by crudités and serve at once. This avocado mixture may also be served as a dip with crisps and small cheese biscuits.

TOMATO CREAM POTS

SERVES 4
350 g (12 oz) small tomatoes
25 g (1 oz) mature Cheddar cheese
25 g (1 oz) grated Parmesan cheese
1 teaspoon chopped fresh basil or marjoram
150 ml (¹/₄ pint) whipping cream
salt and pepper
sprigs of fresh basil or marjoram

Preparation time: 10 minutes
Cooking time: 15 minutes
Preheat the oven to 190°C/375°F/Gas mark 5.

Lightly grease four individual fireproof dishes. Cut the tomatoes in half crosswise and arrange cut-side up in the dishes. Grate the Cheddar cheese and sprinkle the two cheeses over the tomatoes. Sprinkle on the chopped herbs. Lightly season the cream with salt and pepper and pour over the tomatoes. Bake in the oven for 15 minutes. Garnish with a sprig of basil or marjoram and serve at once with wholemeal bread or fingers of crispbread. If liked, a little very finely chopped onion may be sprinkled on the tomatoes before adding the cheese, and chopped chives may then be used for the garnish.

SUMMER VEGETABLE TERRINE

SERVES 4
150 g (6 oz) young carrots
100 g (4 oz) peas
100 g (4 oz) young French beans
100 g (4 oz) fresh spinach leaves
450 g (1 lb) curd or cream cheese
2 eggs
1 garlic clove
grated rind of ¹/₂ lemon
salt and pepper

Preparation time: 20 minutes
Cooking time: 40 minutes

Some of the vegetables may be leftovers, but the terrine is much nicer if everything is freshly cooked. Prepare the terrine a day in advance if possible so that there is plenty of time for it to be chilled and become firm for slicing. Other vegetables may be used if liked, such as sweetcorn kernels, very young thin leeks, strips of celery, or thinly sliced button mushrooms, but do not use too many varieties, and be sure that there is plenty of cheese mixture to separate the differently coloured layers.

Preheat the oven to 160°C/325°C/Gas mark 3.

Cut the carrots in thin lengthwise strips. Trim the tops and the tails of the beans. Cook the carrots, beans and peas separately in salted water until just tender. Drain well and rinse well under cold running water. Blanch the spinach leaves for 30 seconds. Line a 1 kg (2 lb) loaf tin with the spinach leaves, overlapping the edges.

Beat the cheese with a fork until softened and work in the eggs, crushed garlic, lemon rind and plenty of salt and pepper. Spread a 2.5 cm (1 inch) layer of the cheese mixture in the base of the lined loaf tin. Put in the beans, arranging them lengthwise in the tin. Add another layer of cheese mixture, then carrot strips arranged lengthwise. Cover with cheese again, and then add the peas in a layer. Finish with a layer of cheese mixture. Fold over the spinach leaves to enclose the mixture completely.

Cover with a piece of kitchen foil, and place the loaf tin in a roasting tin with enough boiling water to come half-way up the loaf tin. Cook for 40 minutes. Remove the loaf tin from the water and leave until cool. Place in the refrigerator for at least 4 hours, or overnight if possible. Turn on to a serving dish, and serve in thick slices, with thin slices of crisp fresh toast.

STILTON PEARS

SERVES 4
50 g (2 oz) Stilton cheese
50 g (2 oz) natural yogurt
100 g (4 oz) curd cheese
salt and pepper
2 ripe eating pears

Garnish:
shredded lettuce leaves
1 tablespoon chopped fresh chives

Preparation time: 10 minutes

Put the Stilton cheese into a bowl and break up with a fork. Add 1 tablespoon yogurt and mash with cheese. Put the curd cheese into another bowl and beat with the remaining yogurt and plenty of salt and pepper to taste. Peel the pears and cut in half lengthwise. Scoop out the cores and discard. Divide the Stilton mixture between the four pear halves and place in the cavity of each one.

Put a little shredded lettuce on each plate and put a pear half on each one, cut-side down. Spoon over the yogurt mixture and sprinkle with chives. If possible, chill for 30 minutes before serving.

AVOCADOS WITH CURRY CREAM

SERVES 4
2 ripe avocados
juice of $^1/_2$ lemon

Curry Cream:
150 ml ($^1/_4$ pint) double cream
150 ml ($^1/_4$ pint) mayonnaise
2 teaspoons curry paste
1 garlic clove
salt and pepper
2 hard-boiled eggs
1 tablespoon chopped fresh parsley

Garnish:
lemon slices
parsley sprigs

Preparation time: 10 minutes
Chilling time: 4–5 hours

Prepare the curry cream first. Whip the cream lightly and fold in the mayonnaise, curry paste, crushed garlic, salt and pepper. Cover and put into the refrigerator for 4–5 hours so that the flavour mellows. Remove from refrigerator and fold in chopped eggs and parsley. Just before serving, cut the avocados in half lengthwise and discard the stones. Sprinkle the cut surfaces with lemon juice. Place an avocado half on each serving plate and spoon the curry cream into each cavity. Garnish with lemon slices and parsley sprigs and serve at once with thin brown bread and butter.

COTTAGE CHEESE MOUSSE

SERVES 4
450 g (1 lb) cottage cheese
150 ml ($^1/_4$ pint) natural yogurt
1 tablespoon tomato paste
squeeze of lemon juice
salt and pepper

Garnish:
4 peeled thin cucumber slices
1 teaspoon chopped fresh chives
$^1/_2$ teaspoon chopped fresh mint
$^1/_2$ teaspoon paprika

Preparation time: 10 minutes

Put the cottage cheese and yogurt into a bowl and mix well together with a fork. Add tomato paste and lemon juice and season well with salt and pepper. Mix very well and spoon into 4 individual ramekins, pressing down well. Chill in the refrigerator for 1 hour. Just before serving, place a cucumber slice on top of each mousse. Sprinkle with chives and mint, and then with paprika. Serve with Melba toast.

MUSHROOM FRITTERS WITH GARLIC MAYONNAISE

SERVES 4–6
450 g (1 lb) button mushrooms
100 g (4 oz) plain flour
pinch of salt
150 ml (¹/₄ pint) water
1 tablespoon oil
2 egg whites
oil for frying

Garlic Mayonnaise:
8 tablespoons mayonnaise
2 garlic cloves
2 tablespoons chopped fresh parsley
1 tablespoon chopped fresh chives

Preparation time: 10 minutes
Cooking time: 15 minutes

Do not wash the mushrooms or peel them, but wipe them clean and dry with kitchen paper. Sieve the flour into a bowl with the salt and gradually beat in the water and oil. Whisk the egg whites to stiff peaks and fold into the mixture. Heat a pan of deep oil to 190°C/375°F. Drop the mushrooms into the batter and then lift them a few at a time with a slotted spoon and drop into the hot oil. Fry until golden and crisp. Lift out and drain well on kitchen paper. Keep hot while frying the remaining mushrooms.

While the mushrooms are cooking, mix the mayonnaise, crushed garlic and herbs and put into a serving bowl. Serve with the hot mushrooms.

MAIN DISHES

T he main dish of a meal which does not include meat, poultry, game or fish, needs to be not only filling and sustaining, but nourishing and full of flavour and colour as well. A choice can be made from dishes based on grains, beans or pulses, from flans and pasta, from stuffed vegetables and baked or roast meal-in-one combinations. These may most easily be accompanied by a salad or plainly cooked vegetables. New wholemeal or crusty white bread, garlic bread or crisp bread are other good accompaniments.

VEGETABLE PUFF

SERVES 4
1 small onion
1 garlic clove
1 stick celery
2 tablespoons oil
100 g (4 oz) button mushrooms
2 tablespoons plain flour
150 ml ($^1/_4$ pint) vegetable stock or water
1 tablespoon tomato purée
225 g (8 oz) tomatoes
1 small cauliflower
1 tablespoon chopped fresh parsley
$^1/_4$ teaspoon chopped fresh basil
salt and pepper
350 g (12 oz) puff pastry
beaten egg to glaze

Preparation time: 20 minutes
Cooking time: 30 minutes
Preheat the oven to 200°C/400°F/Gas mark 6.

Chop the onion finely. Crush the garlic and slice the celery finely. Heat the oil in a frying pan and cook the onion, garlic and celery over low heat for 5 minutes until soft. Slice the mushrooms and add to the pan. Cook for 1 minute. Stir in the flour and gradually add the stock or water and the tomato purée. Stir well and bring to the boil. Skin the tomatoes, discard seeds, and chop the flesh roughly. Divide the cauliflower into florets and cook in boiling water for 5 minutes, and then chop roughly. Add the tomato and cauliflower pieces to the other vegetables and stir in the herbs and plenty of salt and pepper.

Roll out the pastry into a 35 cm (14 inch) square. Spread the cooked vegetable filling over the pastry, leaving a 2.5 cm (1 inch) border round the edge. Brush the border with beaten egg and carefully roll up the pastry like a Swiss roll. Lift on to a baking sheet which has been rinsed in cold water but not dried (this helps the pastry to puff up). Brush with beaten egg to glaze and cut three or four diagonal slits along the top of the roll of pastry. Bake for 30 minutes. Cut into slices and serve with a green salad.

PISSALADIERE

SERVES 6–8
350 g (12 oz) prepared shortcrust pastry (see page 86)
8 tablespoons olive oil
900 g (2 lb) onions
3 garlic cloves
6 large tomatoes
salt and pepper
10 black olives

Preparation time: 15 minutes
Cooking time: 1 hour 5 minutes
Preheat the oven to 200°C/400°F/Gas mark 6.

Line a 22.5 cm (9 inch) flan tin with pastry and chill for 10 minutes. Prick the pastry well with a fork and press a piece of foil into the tin. Bake for 15 minutes, remove foil and leave to cool.

Meanwhile, heat the oil in a large pan and add finely chopped onions and crushed garlic. Cook over low heat, stirring often, for at least 30 minutes until the onions are very soft. Skin the tomatoes and discard the seeds. Chop the flesh roughly. Add to the onions and continue cooking for 10 minutes. Season very well with salt and pepper. Spread the mixture in the pastry cases. Stone the olives and cut them in half. Arrange on top of the onion mixture. Bake for 25 minutes, and serve hot or cold.

SPINACH ROULADE

SERVES 4
450 g (1 lb) fresh spinach leaves
4 eggs
pinch of ground nutmeg
salt and pepper
25 g (1 oz) vegetable margarine
1 large onion
100 g (4 oz) button mushrooms
25 g (1 oz) plain flour
300 ml (^{1}/$_2$ pint) milk
1 teaspoon lemon juice
1 tablespoon grated Parmesan cheese

Preparation time: 20 minutes
Cooking time: 20 minutes
Preheat the oven to 200°C/400°F/Gas mark 6.

Line a 32.5 cm x 22.5 cm (13 x 9 inches) roasting tin with baking parchment so that it comes above the sides of the pan. Wash the spinach very well and strip the leaves from the thick stems. Put into a large heavy-based pan and cook gently in the water which is on the leaves for 5 minutes. Drain very thoroughly, pressing out excess liquid, and chop the spinach finely. Put into a bowl with the egg yolks, nutmeg, salt and pepper and beat well until thoroughly mixed. Whisk the egg whites to stiff peaks and fold into the spinach mixture. Spread lightly in the prepared tin and bake for 15 minutes until well-risen and firm, and just beginning to brown lightly.

While the roulade is cooking, prepare the filling. Melt the margarine and add thinly sliced onion, cooking gently for 5 minutes. Slice the mushrooms and add to the pan. Continue cooking gently for 2 minutes. Stir in the flour and cook for 1 minute stirring all the time. Take off the heat and gradually stir in the milk. Return to the heat and simmer until thick and smooth, stirring well all the time. Add the lemon juice and season well with salt and pepper.

Take a piece of greaseproof paper and sprinkle with Parmesan cheese. Turn the cooked roulade on to this and peel off the lining paper from the base of the roulade. Quickly spread over the hot sauce, leaving a 2.5 cm (1 inch) border round the edge. Using the paper to ease the roulade over the filling, roll up gently like a Swiss roll. Lift carefully on to a warm serving dish and serve at once in thick slices. Do not worry if the spinach casing cracks slightly during the rolling-up process, but just keep working quickly.

HERBED NUT ROAST

SERVES 4–6
100 g (4 oz) hazelnuts
100 g (4 oz) wholemeal bread
100 g (4 oz) vegetable margarine
400 g (1 lb) onions
1 tablespoon yeast extract
100 g (4 oz) unsalted peanuts
2 tablespoons chopped fresh mixed herbs
2 tablespoons chopped fresh parsley
salt and pepper

Preparation time: 10 minutes
Cooking time: 40 minutes
Preheat the oven to 180°C/350°F/Gas mark 4.

Put the hazelnuts into a blender or food processor. Break the bread into small pieces. Process until the bread forms coarse crumbs (this will only take a few seconds). Melt the margarine in a large pan add the finely chopped onions. Cook gently, stirring well, for 10 minutes until the onion pieces are soft. Stir in the yeast extract. Take off the heat and stir in the hazelnuts and breadcrumbs, peanuts, herbs and plenty of salt and pepper.

Press the mixture lightly into a 900 ml (1 ¹/₂ pint) ovenware dish. Bake for 40 minutes until lightly browned. Serve hot with vegetables or salad. If liked, walnuts, pecans or cashew nuts can be used instead of the peanuts.

PILAF WITH VEGETABLE KEBABS

SERVES 4

Pilaf:
100 g (4 oz) onion
2 celery sticks
2 tablespoons oil
225 g (8 oz) brown rice
600 ml (1 pint) vegetable stock
50 g (2 oz) dried apricots
50 g (2 oz) walnut kernels
50 g (2 oz) seedless raisins
1 cinnamon stick
1 bay-leaf
salt and pepper

Kebabs:
225 g (8 oz) courgettes
8 small tomatoes
1 large onion
8 button mushrooms
1 green pepper
1 tablespoon oil
1 tablespoon lemon juice
1 tablespoon fresh thyme leaves
salt and pepper

Preparation time: 15 minutes
Cooking time: 40 minutes

Prepare the pilaf first. Chop the onion finely and slice the celery finely. Heat the oil in a large frying pan and add the onion and celery. Fry gently for 5 minutes, stirring well, until golden. Add the rice and cook for 1 minute, stirring all the time. Pour on the stock, and stir well. Chop the apricots and walnuts roughly and add to the pan with the raisins. Bring to the boil, stirring occasionally. Add the cinnamon stick, bay-leaf and plenty of salt and pepper. Lower the heat and cover the pan, and simmer for 30 minutes until the rice is just tender and the liquid has been absorbed.

Meanwhile, prepare the kebabs. Do not peel the courgettes, but cut them into thick slices. Leave the tomatoes whole. Cut the onion into eight wedges. Keep the mushrooms whole. Remove core, seeds and membranes from the green pepper, and cut the flesh into eight pieces. Thread the vegetables on to four long metal kebab skewers, alternating the different vegetables. Mix the oil, lemon juice, thyme and plenty of salt and pepper. Brush the vegetables with the oil and lemon mixture and cook under a medium grill, or on a barbecue for 5–10 minutes. Turn the skewers from time to time and brush with the oil and lemon mixture. Serve at once with the pilaf. The pilaf is a useful basic accompaniment to barbecued foods and to plainly grilled meat, poultry, game or fish, and will be enjoyed by the whole family.

FARMHOUSE BEANS

SERVES 4
225 g (8 oz) dried butter or haricot beans
2 celery sticks
50 g (2 oz) onion
1 bay-leaf
pinch of bicarbonate of soda
40 g (1 ¹/₂ oz) vegetable margarine

40 g (1 ¹/₂ oz) plain flour
450 ml (³/₄ pint) milk
50 g (2 oz) grated Cheddar cheese
pinch of ground nutmeg
salt and pepper
2 tomatoes
1 tablespoon chopped fresh parsley

Preparation time: 10 minutes
Soaking time: overnight
Cooking time: 1 hour

Cover the beans with cold water and leave to soak overnight. Drain well and put into a pan, and cover with fresh cold water. Chop the celery and onion and add to the pan with the bay-leaf and soda. Bring to the boil and simmer for 1 hour. Drain very well and discard the bay-leaf.

While the beans are cooking, prepare the rest of the dish. Melt the margarine and stir in the flour. Cook for 1 minute and then gradually stir in the milk and cook gently until smooth and creamy. Take off the heat, and stir in the cheese, nutmeg and plenty of salt and pepper. Mix sauce with the beans and put into an ovenware serving dish. Slice the tomatoes and arrange on top and put under a medium grill until golden. Sprinkle with parsley and serve at once. If liked, some grated Parmesan cheese, or a mixture of grated cheese and breadcrumbs, may be sprinkled on top before grilling, to give a sharper flavour and greater texture.

HONEY-BAKED BEANS

SERVES 4
225 g (8 oz) dried haricot beans
3 tomatoes
50 g (2 oz) onion
50 g (2 oz) honey
1 tablespoon black treacle
1 teaspoon French mustard
salt and pepper
2 tablespoons olive oil

Preparation time: 10 minutes
Soaking time: overnight
Cooking time: 3 hours

Soak the beans in cold water overnight. Drain well and put into a pan with cold water. Simmer for about 1 hour until tender but not broken. Drain very thoroughly. Preheat the oven to 150°C/300°F/Gas mark 2.

Skin the tomatoes and cut into quarters, discarding the seeds. Chop the onion finely. Mix together the beans with the onion pieces, honey, treacle, mustard, salt and pepper. Put into a well-greased ovenware dish and pour on the oil. Cover and bake. Serve as an accompaniment or as a complete meal with tomato sauce and wholemeal bread.

HUNGARIAN BEANS

SERVES 4
350 g (12 oz) haricot beans
75 g (3 oz) onion
1 garlic clove
2 tablespoons oil
1 tablespoon paprika
2 tablespoons tomato paste
1 red pepper
450 g (1 lb) canned tomatoes
150 ml (¹/₄ pint) water
salt and pepper
4 tablespoons soured cream

Preparation time: 10 minutes
Soaking time: overnight
Cooking time: 1 hour

Cover the beans with cold water and leave to soak overnight. Drain well and cook in boiling water for 45 minutes until just tender. Drain very well. Slice the onion thinly and crush the garlic. Heat the oil and add the onion and garlic and cook over low heat for 5 minutes. Stir in the paprika and continue cooking and stirring for 5 minutes. Add the drained beans, tomato paste, chopped pepper, tomatoes in their juice and the water. Bring to the boil, cover and simmer gently for 10 minutes. Season to taste with salt and pepper and stir in the cream just before serving.

CARROT AND CREAM CHEESE QUICHE

SERVES 6
450 g (1 lb) carrots
350 g (12 oz) prepared shortcrust pastry (see page 86)
2 eggs
6 tablespoons single cream
225 g (8 oz) cream cheese
1 tablespoon lemon juice
1 teaspoon chopped fresh thyme

25 g (1 oz) chopped mixed nuts
salt and pepper
25 g (1 oz) grated Parmesan cheese

Preparation time: 20 minutes
Cooking time: 40 minutes
Preheat the oven to 200°C/400°F/Gas mark 6.

Clean the carrots and cut them into small pieces. Cook in boiling salted water until tender. Drain very well and make into a purée in a blender or food processor, leaving the mixture in the goblet.

Line a 22.5 cm (9 inch) flan tin with pastry, and chill for 10 minutes. Prick the pastry well with a fork and press a piece of foil into the tin. Bake for 15 minutes, remove foil and leave to cool.

Add the eggs, cream, cream cheese and lemon juice to the carrots and process until smooth and creamy. Stir in the herbs and nuts and season well with salt and pepper. Pour into the pastry case, sprinkle with Parmesan cheese and bake for 25 minutes. Serve hot or cold.

SAGE AND ONION FLAN

SERVES 4–6
225 g (8 oz) prepared shortcrust pastry (see page 86)
225 g (8 oz) onions
25 g (1 oz) vegetable margarine
150 ml (1/4 pint) milk or creamy milk
1 egg
25 g (1 oz) grated Cheddar cheese
1 tablespoon chopped fresh sage
1 teaspoon chopped fresh parsley
salt and pepper
25 g (1 oz) grated Parmesan cheese

Preparation time: 15 minutes
Cooking time: 35 minutes
Preheat the oven to 200°C/400°F/Gas mark 6.

While the oven is heating put in a baking sheet so that it becomes very hot. Line a 17.5 cm (7 inch) sandwich tin with pastry. Chop the onions finely and toss in the hot margarine for 3–4 minutes until soft and golden. Put the onions into a bowl and stir in the milk, beaten egg, Cheddar cheese, herbs and plenty of salt and pepper. Pour into the pastry case and sprinkle with the Parmesan cheese. Put into the oven at once, placing the flan on the very hot baking sheet (this will help to seal and crisp the pastry case). Bake for 35 minutes. Serve warm with salad.

LEEK PUDDING

SERVES 4
2 large leeks
100 g (4 oz) plain flour
¹/₂ teaspoon baking powder
¹/₄ teaspoon salt
40 g (1 ¹/₂ oz) shredded vegetarian suet

Preparation time: 10 minutes
Cooking time: 2 hours

Trim the roots and green tops from the leeks and discard them. Cut each leek in half lengthwise and wash very thoroughly before chopping into small pieces. Sieve the flour with the baking powder and salt, and stir in the suet and leek pieces. Add just enough cold water to make a fairly stiff consistency which drops from a spoon when shaken. Mix very lightly and put into a greased 600 ml (1 pint) pudding basin.

Cover the basin with a piece of greased greaseproof paper and then a piece of kitchen foil, tying firmly. Take a large heavy-based pan and put in a trivet or upside-down saucer. Put the pudding basin on top of this and pour in boiling water to come half-way up the basin. Cover and simmer for 2 hours, topping up the water occasionally with more boiling water so that the pan does not become dry. Turn out on to a warm serving dish and cut into slices to serve with cheese sauce (see page 37). This also makes a good accompaniment to slices of meat or chicken.

SPECIAL CAULIFLOWER CHEESE

SERVES 4
450 g (1 lb) cauliflower florets
100 g (4 oz) onion
1 tablespoon seasoned flour
1 tablespoon oil
25 g (1 oz) vegetable margarine
25 g (1 oz) plain flour
450 ml (³/₄ pint) milk or creamy milk
50 g (2 oz) grated Cheddar cheese
25 g (1 oz) flaked almonds
salt and pepper
pinch of ground paprika
25 g (1 oz) wholemeal breadcrumbs
25 g (1 oz) grated Parmesan cheese
1 tablespoon chopped fresh parsley

Preparation time: 10 minutes
Cooking time: 30 minutes
Preheat the oven to 200°C/400°F/Gas mark 6.

Cook the cauliflower florets in boiling salted water until tender but unbroken and drain very well. Put them into a greased ovenware dish. Slice the onion into very thin rings, and dip them into seasoned flour. Fry in the oil until crisp and golden. Drain well, saving the oil.

Melt the margarine and stir in the flour. Cook for 1 minute and then gradually stir in the milk. Cook over low heat, stirring well, until the sauce is creamy. Remove from the heat and stir in the Cheddar cheese and half the onion rings. Cook the almonds in the remaining oil until just golden, and stir into the sauce, with the salt and pepper. Pour over the cauliflower and sprinkle with paprika. Bake for 15 minutes, under a covering of foil. Remove the foil and cover the surface with the remaining onions. Mix the breadcrumbs and Parmesan cheese and sprinkle on top. Bake for 5 minutes. Sprinkle with parsley and serve at once.

BAKED AUBERGINES WITH CREAM CHEESE

SERVES 4
2 large aubergines
salt
50 g (2 oz) vegetable margarine
2 tablespoons oil
100 g (4 oz) onion
350 g (12 oz) tomatoes
1 teaspoon chopped fresh basil
1 tablespoon chopped fresh parsley
pepper
150 g (6 oz) cream cheese
3 tablespoons milk
25 g (1 oz) dry breadcrumbs
25 g (1 oz) grated Parmesan cheese

Preparation time: 40 minutes
Cooking time: 40 minutes

Wash and dry the aubergines but do not peel. Cut across in thick slices. Arrange in a colander, sprinkle with salt and leave to drain for 30 minutes. Rinse in cold water and pat dry with kitchen paper.

Preheat the oven to 180°C/350°F/Gas mark 4. Heat the margarine and oil together in a frying pan and fry the aubergine slices until golden on both sides. Drain well and keep on one side. Slice the onion thinly and cook in the fat for 5 minutes until soft and golden. Peel the tomatoes, discard the seeds and chop the flesh roughly. Add to the onion with the herbs, salt and pepper and cook gently for 10 minutes.

Divide the aubergine slices into three portions and put one layer in a greased ovenware dish. Cover with half the tomato and onion mixture.

Cream the cream cheese and milk together and spread half on top of the tomato mixture. Add another layer of aubergines and the remaining tomato mixture. Spread on remaining cream cheese and finish with a layer of aubergine slices. Mix the breadcrumbs and cheese and sprinkle on the surface. Bake for 40 minutes until golden brown and bubbling. Serve hot with a green salad and wholemeal bread.

LENTIL KEDGEREE

SERVES 4
225 g (8 oz) red lentils
750 ml (1 ¹/₂ pints) water
1 bay-leaf
225 g (8 oz) long-grain brown rice
225 g (8 oz) onion
50 g (2 oz) vegetable margarine
1 garlic clove
2 teaspoons curry powder
2 teaspoons lemon juice

Preparation time: 10 minutes
Cooking time: 50 minutes

Cover the lentils with the water and add the bay-leaf, and simmer gently until they make a thick soft purée. Discard the bay-leaf and keep the lentils warm. Meanwhile, cook the rice in boiling salted water for about 40 minutes until tender and drain well. Rinse in cold water and put into an ovenware dish in a low oven to keep warm.

Chop the onion finely and cook in the margarine for 5 minutes until softened. Crush the garlic and add to the onions with the curry powder. Continue cooking for 5 minutes, stirring well. Mix the lentils into the warm rice very gently with a fork, and add the onions. Season well with salt and pepper and the lemon juice. Serve hot.

Kedgeree is now usually made with fish and rice, but lentils make a dish which is closer to the Indian original. If liked, add some cooked peas, sliced cooked mushrooms or chopped peppers, or chopped hard-boiled eggs. A tomato salad or green salad may be served with the dish.

VEGETABLE SAMOSAS

SERVES 6

Filling:
900 g (2 lb) cooked mixed vegetables
100 g (4 oz) onion

1 garlic clove
25 g (1 oz) vegetable margarine
1 teaspoon ground ginger
1 teaspoon ground cumin
1 teaspoon coriander
$1/2$ teaspoon mustard powder
salt and pepper

Pastry:
225 g (8oz) plain wholemeal flour
$1/2$ teaspoon baking powder
$1/2$ teaspoon salt
50 g (2 oz) vegetable margarine
oil for deep frying

Preparation time: 20 minutes
Cooking time: 20 minutes

Make a good selection of cooked vegetables which may include potatoes, peas, carrots and swedes. If liked, add some sweetcorn kernels or some beansprouts. Chop large vegetables into small cubes. Chop the onion finely and crush the garlic. Cook in the margarine over low heat for 10 minutes. Stir in the spices and plenty of salt and pepper. Add the vegetables and stir well so they are coated in spices. Remove from heat and leave until cold.

To make the pastry, stir the flour, baking powder and salt together and rub in the fat until the mixture is like fine breadcrumbs. Add 6–7 tablespoons cold water to make a soft but not sticky dough. Knead the dough on a floured surface for 5 minutes so that it becomes very pliable. Divide into 16 equal-sized pieces and form into balls. Roll the balls very thinly with a rolling pin so that each one is about 15 cms (6 inch) diameter. Cut each circle in half with a sharp knife.

Put a heaped teaspoonful of filling in the centre of each piece of pastry. Brush the edges with a little water and fold in the corners to make small triangular packages, pressing the edges together firmly. Deep-fry a few at a time until crisp and golden. Drain very well and serve hot or cold.

VEGETABLE CURRY

SERVES 4
225 g (8 oz) onion
1 garlic clove
1 cooking apple
2.5 cm (1 inch) fresh ginger
2 tablespoons oil

1 tablespoon white mustard seeds
1 teaspoon ground turmeric
1 teaspoon ground cumin
1/2 teaspoon ground fenugreek
1/4 teaspoon mild chili powder
450 ml (3/4 pint) vegetable stock
1/2 lemon
salt and pepper
225 g (8 oz) potatoes
225 g (8 oz) carrots
225 g (8 oz) cauliflower florets
225 g (8 oz) runner beans
50 g (2 oz) sultanas
50 g (2 oz) salted peanuts
1 tablespoon desiccated coconut

Preparation time: 15 minutes
Cooking time: 30 minutes

This recipe has a fresh, spicy flavour, but if all the spices are not obtainable, use 1–2 tablespoons curry powder. Chop the onion finely and crush the garlic. Peel, core and chop the apple. Peel and grate the ginger. Heat the oil and cook the onion, garlic, apple and ginger for 5 minutes over low heat, stirring gently. Add the mustard seeds, turmeric, coriander, cumin, fenugreek, and chili powder. Cook gently for 3 minutes. Add the stock and bring to the boil. Grate the lemon rind and squeeze out the juice. Add the rind and the juice to the pan with salt and pepper. Cover and simmer for 2 minutes.

Peel the potatoes and cut them into dice. Slice the carrots thinly. Skin the tomatoes and discard the seeds. Chop the flesh roughly. Slice the runner beans. Add the potatoes, carrots and tomatoes to the pan and simmer for 10 minutes. Add cauliflower, beans, sultanas and peanuts. Cover and simmer for 10 minutes until the vegetables are tender but not broken. Serve sprinkled with coconut. If liked, hard-boiled eggs may be served with this curry. The mixture is also good if allowed to become cold and served with a salad.

COTTAGE HOTPOT

SERVES 4–6
450 g (1 lb) potatoes
225 g (8 oz) onions
225 g (8 oz) carrots
225 g (8 oz) parsnips
225 g (8 oz) Jerusalem artichokes
2 celery sticks

100 g (4 oz) walnut pieces
100 g (4 oz) Cheddar pieces
1 tablespoon fresh rosemary leaves
salt and pepper
450 ml ($^3/_4$ pint) vegetable stock

Preparation time: 20 minutes
Cooking time: 1 $^1/_2$ hours
Preheat the oven to 190°C/375°F/Gas mark 5.

Peel the potatoes and slice thinly. Peel all the other root vegetables and slice thinly. Slice the celery sticks. Put half the potato slices in the bottom of a greased casserole. Add the remaining vegetables in layers, sprinkling each layer with nuts, three-quarters of the grated cheese, rosemary and plenty of salt and pepper. Finish with a layer of potatoes arranged neatly on top and sprinkle with remaining cheese. Pour on the stock. Cover and bake for 1 hour. Remove the lid and continue baking for 30 minutes until golden brown.

STUFFED MARROW RINGS

SERVES 4
900 g (2 lb) vegetable marrow
75 g (3 oz) onion
150 g (6 oz) button mushrooms
1 tablespoon oil
25 g (1 oz) wholemeal breadcrumbs
1 tablespoon chopped fresh marjoram
1 tablespoon chopped fresh parsley
salt and pepper
50 g (2 oz) Cheddar cheese

Preparation time: 15 minutes
Cooking time: 30 minutes
Preheat the oven to 180°C/350°F/Gas Mark 4.

This recipe may be used with courgettes instead of marrow. Use 2 small courgettes for each person and cut lengthwise, scooping out centres to fill with stuffing.

Do not peel the marrow but slice across in 5 cm (2 inch) rings and discard seeds. Arrange in a single layer in a greased baking dish. Chop the onion and mushroom finely. Heat the oil and cook the onion over low heat for 5 minutes. Stir in the mushrooms and continue cooking for 3 minutes. Take off the heat and stir in the breadcrumbs, herbs and plenty of salt and pepper. Mix well and fill the centre of each marrow ring or halved courgette. Cover with foil and bake for 10 minutes. Remove foil and sprinkle with cheese and continue baking for 20 minutes.

GREEK BEAN MOUSSAKA

SERVES 6
225 g (8 oz) dried beans
100 ml (1 pint) water
175 g (6 oz) onions
2 celery sticks
1 large carrot
4 tablespoons oil
100 g (4 oz) mushrooms
4 tomatoes
1 tablespoon tomato paste
1 teaspoon of chopped fresh marjoram
salt and pepper
1 bay-leaf
675 g (1 1/2 lb) aubergines

Cheese Sauce:
25 g (1 oz) vegetable margarine
25 g (1 oz) plain flour
300 ml (1/2 pint) milk
100 g (4 oz) Cheddar cheese
1 egg
pinch of ground nutmeg
salt and pepper

Preparation time: 20 minutes
Soaking time: overnight
Cooking time: 3 1/2 hours

Use any type of dried bean, or a mixture of them. Cover with the water and leave to soak overnight. Drain the beans, cover with fresh water and simmer for about 2 hours until tender (the time will depend on the type of beans used, and their age). Drain and reserve 300 ml (1/2 pint) cooking liquid.

Meanwhile, prepare the remaining ingredients. Chop the onion finely. Slice the celery, carrot and mushrooms thinly. Heat the oil and add the onion, celery and carrot. Cook gently for 5 minutes, stirring well. Add the mushrooms and continue cooking for 2 minutes. Stir in the reserved cooking liquid. Skin the tomatoes and discard seeds. Chop the flesh roughly and add to the pan with the tomato paste, marjoram, salt, pepper and bay-leaf. Bring to the boil stirring well. Add the beans, cover and simmer for about 30 minutes until the beans are very soft and most of the liquid has been absorbed, leaving a moist mixture. Discard the bay-leaf.

While the beans are cooking, slice the aubergines across thinly. Sprinkle with salt and leave to stand for about 1 hour. Drain well and rinse under running water. Pat dry with kitchen paper and arrange in a single layer in a grill pan. Brush very lightly with oil and grill under medium heat until lightly brown on both sides.

Preheat the oven to 180°C/350°F/Gas mark 4.

Make the sauce by melting the margarine and working in the flour. Cook over low heat for 1 minute and gradually work in the milk. Bring to the boil, stirring all the time. Take off the heat and stir in the cheese little by little and finally the beaten egg. Season well with nutmeg, salt and pepper,

Grease an ovenware dish and arrange one-third of the aubergine slices in the bottom. Top with half of the bean mixture, then another third aubergine slices. Add remaining beans and top with aubergine slices. Pour over the cheese sauce. Bake for 30 minutes until golden brown and serve at once with a green salad.

NUTTY CHEESEBURGERS

SERVES 4
150 g (6 oz) walnut or pecan kernels
50 g (2 oz) wholemeal bread
100 g (4 oz) grated Cheddar cheese
50 g (2 oz) onion
salt and pepper
1 egg
1 tablespoon tomato purée
oil for shallow frying

Preparation time: 10 minutes
Cooking time: 5–10 minutes

Reserve 50 g (2 oz) walnuts or pecans. Put the rest into a blender or food processor with pieces of bread until the bread forms coarse crumbs. Put the processed nuts and breadcrumbs into a bowl and add the cheese. Grate the onion coarsely and add to the bowl. Season well with salt and pepper and mix with the egg and tomato purée until well blended.

Divide the mixture into quarters and shape into 4 burgers about 1.25 cm (1 inch) thick. Chop the reserved nuts and press into the burgers. Shallow-fry in oil for about 5 minutes until brown on both sides, turning once. Alternatively, put the burgers on to a lightly greased baking sheet and bake at 200°C/400°F/Gas mark 6 for 20 minutes. Serve hot or cold with vegetables, baked beans or salad, or in burger buns with pickles, or tomato ketchup.

LENTIL BURGERS WITH YOGURT SAUCE

SERVES 6
75 g (3 oz) onion
1 garlic clove
1 celery stick
1 medium carrot
2 tablespoons oil
225 g (8 oz) brown lentils
salt and pepper
4 level tablespoons wholemeal flour
1 tablespoon mango chutney
1 teaspoon curry powder
$^1/_2$ teaspoon ground cumin
$^1/_2$ teaspoon ground ginger

Yogurt Sauce:
150 ml ($^1/_2$ pint) natural yogurt
1 garlic clove
1 tablespoon chopped fresh parsley

Preparation time: 15 minutes
Cooking time: 1 $^1/_2$ hours

Chop the onion finely and crush the garlic. Slice the celery thinly and then chop finely. Scrape or peel the carrot and chop finely. Heat the oil and cook the vegetables over a low heat for 5 minutes. Add the lentils with 450 ml ($^3/_4$ pint) water, salt and pepper and bring to the boil. Cover and simmer for 1–1 $^1/_2$ hours until the lentils are soft and the liquid has been absorbed. Add half the flour, the chutney and spices and mix well. Cook gently for 3 minutes, stirring all the time. Taste and add more salt and pepper if liked. Remove from the heat and leave until cool enough to handle.

Divide the mixture into 18 pieces and shape into burgers about 1.25 cm ($^1/_2$ inch) thick. Coat with the remaining flour and fry in hot shallow oil until crisp and golden on both sides. Make the sauce by mixing the yogurt, crushed garlic and parsley together.

Serve on a bed of rice with the dressing served separately, or use the burgers to fill hot wholemeal baps or pitta bread with plenty of salad or chutney.

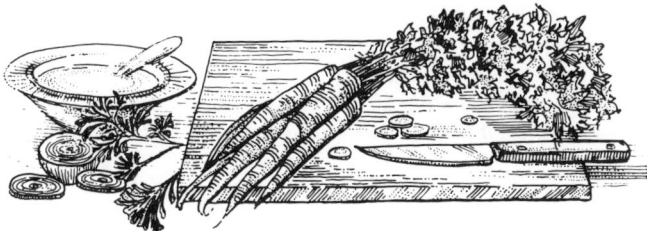

MEDITERRANEAN LENTIL CASSEROLE

SERVES 4
175 g (6 oz) onion
1 garlic clove
2 celery sticks
4 small courgettes
2 tablespoons oil
4 tomatoes
900 ml (1 ¹/₂ pints) water or vegetable stock
salt and pepper
¹/₄ teaspoon ground coriander
225 g (8 oz) brown lentils
2 tablespoons chopped fresh parsley

Preparation time: 10 minutes
Cooking time: 2 hours

Brown lentils do not need soaking. If green or red ones are preferred, check whether they should be soaked before cooking. Chop the onion finely and crush the garlic. Slice the celery and the unpeeled courgettes thinly. Heat the oil in a large pan and add the vegetables. Cook gently for 10 minutes, stirring well until softened.

Peel the tomatoes, cut in quarters and discard the pips. Add to the pan with the water or stock, salt, pepper and coriander, and bring to the boil. Add the lentils, cover and simmer for about 1 ¹/₂ hours until tender. Serve hot, sprinkled with parsley and accompanied by wholemeal or crusty white bread. If it is more convenient, the dish may be cooked at 180°C/350°F/Gas mark 4 for about 2 hours until the lentils are tender.

PASTA RATATOUILLE

SERVES 4–6
1 large onion
1 garlic clove
450 g (1 lb) courgettes
1 large aubergine
1 green pepper
450 g (1 lb) tomatoes
1 tablespoon chopped fresh marjoram
salt and pepper
450 g (1 lb) pasta shapes
1 tablespoon chopped fresh parsley
ground Parmesan cheese for serving

Preparation time: 15 minutes
Cooking time: 30 minutes

Chop the onion finely. Crush the garlic. Do not peel the courgettes or aubergine, but wash and dry them. Slice the courgettes thinly, and dice the aubergine. Cut the pepper in half lengthwise and discard the stalk, seeds and membranes before dicing the flesh. Skin the tomatoes and discard seeds. Chop the flesh roughly and mix with all the other vegetables and marjoram in a large, heavy-based pan. Cover and cook gently for about 30 minutes until the vegetables are tender, stirring occasionally. Add salt and pepper.

While the vegetables are cooking, boil a large pan of salted water and boil the pasta for 15 minutes (only 5 minutes if the pasta is fresh). Drain well and place in a warm serving dish or on individual plates. Adjust the seasoning of the sauce and pour over the pasta. Sprinkle with parsley. Serve at once with Parmesan cheese.

NOODLES WITH MUSHROOM SAUCE

SERVES 4
450 g (1 lb) plain, wholemeal or spinach noodles
salt and pepper
1 garlic clove
175 g (6 oz) button mushrooms
50 g (2 oz) vegetable margarine
150 ml (¹/₄ pint) double cream
2 egg yolks
grated Parmesan cheese

Preparation time: 5 minutes
Cooking time: 15 minutes

Bring a large pan of salted water to the boil. Add the noodles and cook for 10–12 minutes until just tender (wholemeal noodles may need a few minutes longer). Drain very well.

While the pasta is cooking, prepare the sauce. Crush the garlic. Do not peel the mushrooms but wipe them clean and cut into thin slices. Melt the margarine and cook the garlic over low heat for 1 minute. Add the mushrooms and cook gently for 2 minutes. Stir in the cream and simmer very gently for 10 minutes. Season to taste with salt and pepper and remove from the heat. Beat the eggs lightly and stir into the cream sauce. Pour over the noodles and toss well. Serve at once with grated Parmesan cheese.

MUSHROOM RISOTTO

SERVES 4
50 g (2 oz) onion
1 garlic clove
50 g (2 oz) vegetable margarine
350 g (12 oz) risotto rice
300 ml ($^1/_2$ pint) dry white wine
salt and pepper
300 ml ($^1/_2$ pint) vegetable stock
1 bay-leaf
sprig of thyme
sprig of parsley
225 g (8 oz) button mushrooms
pinch of saffron
50 g (2 oz) grated Parmesan cheese

Preparation time: 10 minutes
Cooking time: 30 minutes

If wild mushrooms or Chinese mushrooms are available, use these for the best flavour. If saffron is unavailable, a pinch of turmeric will colour the rice. Chop the onion finely and crush the garlic. Melt the margarine in a heavy-based large frying pan and cook the onion and garlic over low heat for about 10 minutes until soft and golden. Stir in the rice and wine and bring to the boil. Boil hard until the wine has been reduced by half.

Add half the stock, herbs and plenty of salt and pepper. Simmer uncovered for about 15 minutes until the rice is tender and the liquid has been absorbed (it will probably be necessary to add more of the stock during cooking to prevent dryness, as the risotto should be creamy). Slice the mushrooms thinly and stir into the risotto with the saffron. Heat for 5 minutes and serve sprinkled with cheese.

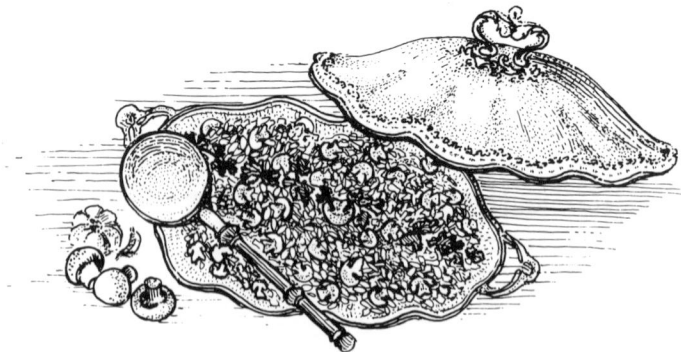

VEGETABLES

egetables can serve two purposes in a non-meat meal. They may of course be plainly steamed or boiled, grilled or roasted to serve as accompaniments to the main course, but they can also be prepared in sauces, as casseroles or as baked dishes to form the centrepiece of a meal. These dishes often serve as a useful introduction to the non-meat diet, for carnivores who will enjoy them served as accompaniments to roast, grilled or cold meats, may often find themselves gradually eliminating the meat factor of their meal.

SWEET AND SOUR RED CABBAGE

SERVES 4
15 g (1/2 oz) vegetable margarine
50 g (2 oz) onion
1 tablespoon dark soft brown sugar
1 tablespoon cider vinegar
900 g (2 lb) red cabbage
salt and pepper
150 ml (1/4 pint) dry cider
1 eating apple

Preparation time: 10 minutes
Cooking time: 2 hours

Melt the margarine in a large saucepan. Chop the onion finely and add to the pan. Cook over low heat for 10 minutes until the onion is soft and golden. Add the sugar and vinegar. Shred the cabbage finely and add to the pan with the salt and pepper and cider. Cover tightly and simmer for 1 hour.

Peel and core the apple and slice it thinly. Stir into the cabbage and continue cooking over low heat for 1 hour. If liked, 1 teaspoon of ground mixed spice may be added with the apple.

WHITE CABBAGE CASSEROLE WITH CARAWAY

SERVES 4
1 firm white cabbage
15 g (1 oz) vegetable margarine
50 g (2 oz) onion
1 small head celery
150 ml (¹/₄ pint) white wine or vegetable stock
1 teaspoon white wine vinegar
salt and pepper
2 teaspoons caraway seeds

Preparation time: 10 minutes
Cooking time: 25 minutes

Shred the cabbage finely and put into a pan of boiling salted water. Boil for 2 minutes and drain very well. Melt the margarine in a shallow pan and add finely sliced onion. Slice the celery finely and add to the pan. Stir well over low heat for 5 minutes. Add the cabbage, wine or stock and vinegar. Season well with salt and pepper and stir in half the caraway seeds. Cover and simmer for 20 minutes. Stir in the remaining caraway seeds.

CABBAGE PROVENÇAL

SERVES 4
1 small green cabbage
50 g (2 oz) onion
150 ml (¹/₄ pint) red wine
salt and pepper
1 garlic clove
1 tablespoon oil
4 tomatoes
1 tablespoon tomato paste
50 g (2 oz) black olives

Preparation time: 10 minutes
Cooking time: 10 minutes

Shred the cabbage coarsely. Chop the onion finely. Put the cabbage and the onion into a pan with the wine, salt and pepper. Cover and bring to the boil and then simmer until the cabbage is just tender. Drain the cabbage well, reserving liquid. Crush the garlic and cook in the oil for 1 minute. Skin the tomatoes and discard the seeds. Chop the flesh roughly and add to the garlic. Add the tomato paste and the cooking liquid and bring to the boil. Stir in the olives and pour over the cabbage. Serve very hot.

BAKED ONIONS WITH CARROT STUFFING

SERVES 4
4 large onions
4 large carrots
50 g (2 oz) vegetable margarine
salt and pepper
25 g (1 oz) plain flour
450 ml (³/₄ pint) milk
75 g (3 oz) fine white or brown breadcrumbs
25 g (1 oz) grated Parmesan cheese
pinch of ground nutmeg

Preparation time: 10 minutes
Cooking time: 45 minutes

Peel the onions and put them into a pan of boiling water. Boil until they are tender. Drain very well and scoop out the centres carefully, reserving the onion pieces. Cook the carrots until tender and chop them into small pieces. Drain and mix with the reserved onion pieces. Melt the margarine and add 1 tablespoon to the vegetables. Season well with salt and pepper and mix thoroughly. Place the whole onions in a greased ovenware dish and fill with the carrot mixture.

Reserve 1 tablespoon melted margarine. Stir the flour into the remaining margarine and cook for 30 seconds over low heat. Work in the milk slowly and stir over low heat until smooth and creamy. Season with salt and pepper and pour over the onions. Sprinkle thickly with breadcrumbs. Top with cheese and a pinch of nutmeg. Put under a hot grill until the breadcrumbs are crisp and lightly browned, and serve at once.

WEST COUNTRY CIDERED CARROTS

SERVES 4
600 ml (1 pint) medium sweet cider
450 g (1 lb) carrots
1 small head celery
salt and pepper
1 tablespoon chopped fresh parsley

Preparation time: 10 minutes
Cooking time: 45 minutes

Put the cider into a large pan and bring to the boil. Cut the carrots and celery into 5 cm (2 inch) lengths, and cut each piece of carrot into four pieces lengthwise. Put the carrots into the cider and simmer for 15 minutes. Add the celery, salt and pepper and cook for 30 minutes.

Drain the vegetables, reserving the liquid, and keep them hot. Boil the cooking liquid until it has reduced to about 4 tablespoonsful. Pour over the vegetables and sprinkle with parsley.

PARISIAN PEAS

SERVES 4–6
900 g (2 lb) fresh peas
12 small white onions
25 g (1 oz) vegetable margarine
1 teaspoon plain flour
300 ml (¹/₂ pint) vegetable stock
2 tablespoons chopped fresh parsley
salt and pepper

Preparation time: 15 minutes
Cooking time: 25 minutes

Shell the peas and keep on one side. If frozen peas are used, about 300 g (10 oz) will be enough. Peel the onions and cook in the margarine over low heat until they begin to soften but do not lose their shape. Work the flour into the mixture and then add the stock. Bring to the boil, cover and simmer until the onions are tender. Add the peas, parsley and plenty of salt and pepper. Cover and simmer for about 15 minutes until the peas are tender.

SWEETCORN FRITTERS

SERVES 4
225 g (8 oz) sweetcorn kernels
100 g (4 oz) plain flour
1 teaspoon baking powder
¹/₂ teaspoon salt
2 eggs
2 tablespoons milk
1 tablespoon melted vegetable margarine
oil for frying

Preparation time: 10 minutes
Cooking time: 10 minutes

The sweetcorn kernels may be frozen or canned, or cut from a freshly-cooked cob. Thaw the frozen variety, or drain the canned corn thoroughly. Sieve together the flour, baking powder and salt. Beat the eggs and milk together and then gradually beat into the flour mixture. Add the sweetcorn kernels and melted margarine and mix well.

Heat the oil in a thick frying pan and fry tablespoonsful of the mixture until golden on both sides. Drain thoroughly and serve very hot.

CRISPY PARSNIP BALLS

SERVES 4
450 g (1 lb) parsnips
100 g (4 oz) vegetable margarine
1 tablespoon milk
salt and pepper
pinch of ground nutmeg
1 egg
75 g (3 oz) dry breadcrumbs
oil for deep-frying

Preparation time: 10 minutes
Cooking time: 30 minutes

Peel the parsnips and cut into small pieces. Boil until tender and drain very well. Mash with the margarine, milk, salt, pepper and nutmeg. Cook and stir over a low heat until the mixture is thick and creamy. Cool to lukewarm and beat in a little of the egg to give a smooth mixture.

Shape into 16 balls and roll in the remaining beaten egg. Dip into the breadcrumbs until thickly coated. Fry in the oil until golden.

RATATOUILLE

SERVES 4
2 large aubergines
2 large green peppers
3 large onions
3 medium courgettes
4 large tomatoes
2 garlic cloves
4 tablespoons olive oil
salt and pepper
2 tablespoons chopped fresh parsley

Preparation time: 15 minutes
Standing time: 2 hours
Cooking time: 1 hour

Wash and dry the aubergines but do not peel them. Cut across into 1.25 cm ($^1/_2$ inch) slices. Place on a shallow dish and sprinkle with salt. Leave to stand for 2 hours and drain off liquid. Rinse the aubergine pieces in cold water and dry with kitchen paper. Remove seeds from the peppers and cut the flesh into slices. Peel and slice the onions. Slice the courgettes thinly. Peel the tomatoes and discard the seeds. Cut each aubergine slice into four pieces.

Heat the oil in a heavy pan and stir in the aubergine, peppers, onions and courgettes. Cover and simmer for 30 minutes. Add the tomatoes and garlic and season well with salt and pepper. Cover and continue cooking for 30 minutes. Sprinkle with parsley before serving. This is very good hot, but even better if kept for 24 hours and served cold with crusty bread.

COTTAGE POTATO BAKE

SERVES 4
1 garlic clove
675 g (1 ¹/₂ lb) potatoes
50 g (2 oz) grated Cheddar cheese
salt and pepper
pinch of ground nutmeg
300 ml (¹/₂ pint) milk or creamy milk
1 egg
25 g (1 oz) vegetable margarine

Preparation time 10 minutes
Cooking time: 1 ¹/₄ hours
Preheat the oven to 190°C/375°F/Gas mark 5.

Grease an ovenware dish and spread the base with crushed garlic. Peel and slice the potatoes very thinly and put in layers in the dish alternately with layers of grated cheese, salt, pepper and nutmeg. The top layer should be potatoes. Beat the egg and milk together and pour over the potatoes. Place the dish in a roasting tin of hot water to prevent drying out. Bake for 1 hour with a covering of foil. Remove foil and continue baking for 15 minutes to brown the potatoes lightly.

CHINESE STIR-FRY

SERVES 4
1 tablespoon oil
1 large onion
1 garlic clove
1 tablespoon grated fresh root ginger
50 g (2 oz) mushrooms
450 g (1 lb) mange-tout peas
450 g (1 lb) Chinese or hard white cabbage
100 g (4 oz) bean sprouts
50 g (2 oz) unsalted peanuts
1 tablespoon soy sauce

6 tablespoons water or vegetable stock
salt and pepper

Preparation time: 10 minutes
Cooking time: 10 minutes

If a wok is not available, use a large thick frying pan or paella pan. Peel and chop the onion roughly. Do not peel the mushrooms but slice them thinly. Top and tail the mange-tout peas. Shred the cabbage finely. If unsalted peanuts are unobtainable, use the salted variety, but omit any extra salt in the recipe.

Heat the oil in a wok or frying pan and add the onion, crushed garlic, ginger and mushrooms, and fry quickly for 3 minutes, stirring or shaking the vegetables constantly. Add the peas and cabbage and continue cooking for 2 minutes, stirring or shaking. Add the remaining ingredients and cook over moderate heat for 5 minutes until the vegetables are tender but still crisp and most of the liquid has evaporated. Serve at once.

BAKED BEETROOT

SERVES 4–6
18 small beetroot
30 ml (¹/₂ pint) single cream
salt and pepper
50 g (2 oz) grated Parmesan cheese
1 tablespoon chopped fresh chives
25 g (1 oz) vegetable margarine

Preparation time: 10 minutes
Cooking time: 40 minutes
Preheat the oven to 180°C/350°F/Gas mark 4.

Boil the beetroot until tender. Drain and peel and keep whole. Put into a greased ovenware dish. Mix the cream with plenty of salt and pepper, cheese and chives and pour over the beetroot. Cut the margarine into flakes and sprinkle on the surface. Bake for 20 minutes and serve hot.

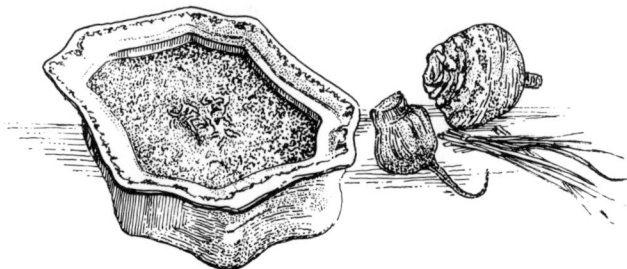

DEVILLED NEW POTATOES

SERVES 4
450 g (1 lb) small new potatoes
25 g (1 oz) vegetable margarine
6 tablespoons whipping cream
1 teaspoon French mustard
$^1/_2$ teaspoon Worcestershire sauce
1 tablespoon chopped fresh chives

Preparation time: 10 minutes
Cooking time: 15 minutes

Scrape the potatoes and cook in boiling salted water until just tender. Drain well and toss with margarine. Mix together the cream, mustard, Worcestershire sauce and chives. Pour over the potatoes and shake the pan gently. Serve at once.

RICH TOMATO SAUCE

MAKES 300 ML ($^1/_2$ PINT)
2 tablespoons oil
1 garlic clove
400 g (14 oz) canned tomatoes
1 tablespoon tomato purée
2 teaspoons sugar
salt and pepper

Preparation time: 5 minutes
Cooking time: 45 minutes

Heat the oil in a heavy-based saucepan and add the garlic clove cut in half. Cook very gently for 5 minutes and discard the garlic. Add the tomatoes with their liquid, tomato purée, sugar, salt and pepper. Bring to the boil, cover and simmer over very low heat for 40 minutes, stirring occasionally. The sauce may be used while still rough textured, or it may be sieved to make a smooth sauce.

Canned tomatoes are quick to use, they also have a greater depth of flavour than most British tomatoes. Sometimes they may be bought canned with herbs and of course these will add yet more flavour to the finished sauce.

SALADS

A salad is much more than just a limp lettuce leaf, plain tomato or cucumber in a vinegary dressing. A combination of raw and/or cooked vegetables may be prepared with an unusual dressing and served as a complete meal-in-one. If eggs and cheese are added, the whole family will also enjoy a salad meal, while cooked grains and pulses are not only tasty but also very nourishing and filling when turned into cold salad.

COURGETTES WITH CAPER DRESSING

SERVES 4
8 medium courgettes
50 g (2 oz) onion
1 garlic clove
6 tablespoons oil
2 tablespoons white wine vinegar
1 tablespoon capers
1 teaspoon chopped fresh parsley
1 teaspoon chopped fresh marjoram
salt and pepper
lettuce leaves

Preparation time: 15 minutes
Standing time: 2 ¹/₂ hours

Wash the courgettes and dry them with kitchen paper. Do not peel but cut across in 1.25 cm (¹/₂ inch) slices. Put into a pan of boiling salted water and simmer for 10 minutes. Drain very well, retaining the liquid. Place the courgettes in a bowl. Chop the onion and garlic very finely and sprinkle over the courgette slices. Mix the oil and vinegar and pour over the courgettes. Cover and leave to stand for 2 hours.

Drain off the liquid from the courgettes and mix with the capers, parsley, marjoram and plenty of salt and pepper. Arrange a bed of lettuce leaves in a serving bowl and put in the courgettes. Pour over the dressing and chill for 30 minutes before serving.

SPANISH POTATO SALAD

SERVES 4
450 g (1 lb) new potatoes
4 tablespoons olive oil
1 tablespoon wine vinegar
2 garlic cloves
1 small red pepper
1 tablespoon chopped fresh chives

Preparation time: 20 minutes

Scrape the potatoes and cook until tender but unbroken. Drain very well and put into a small serving dish. Mix the oil and vinegar and pour over the hot potatoes, tossing them so that they are well coated. Crush the garlic and stir into the bowl. Chop the pepper finely and sprinkle over the potatoes. Sprinkle with chives and serve at once while still warm.

TOMATO AND AVOCADO SALAD

SERVES 4
450 g (1 lb) tomatoes
1 avocado
1 tablespoon lemon juice
6 tablespoons olive oil
3 tablespoons white wine vinegar
1 teaspoon sugar
1 teaspoon made mustard
salt and pepper
6 spring onions

Preparation time: 15 minutes

Skin the tomatoes and cut across in thin slices. Arrange round the edge of a flat serving dish. Peel the avocado and cut in half lengthwise. Remove and discard the stone. Slice the avocado and arrange in the centre of the tomato slices. Sprinkle the avocado with lemon juice and chill while making the dressing. Mix the oil, vinegar, sugar, mustard, salt and pepper. Chop the spring onions finely. Just before serving, pour over the dressing and sprinkle with chives.

For a first course, or as a light meal, arrange some slices of Mozzarella cheese inside the circle of tomatoes before preparing the avocado and dressing.

CRUNCHY WINTER SALAD

SERVES 4–6
350 g (12 oz) hard white cabbage
175 g (6 oz) carrots
1 large green pepper
25 g (1 oz) onion
1 eating apple
1 tablespoon lemon juice
50 g (2 oz) sultanas
50 g (2 oz) chopped mixed nuts
150 ml (¹/₄ pint) mayonnaise (see page 60)

Preparation time: 15 minutes

Shred the cabbage finely and put into a salad bowl. Grate the carrot coarsely and add to the cabbage. Cut the pepper in half and discard the seeds and membrane. Chop the pepper and onion finely and add to the bowl. Wash and dry the apple but do not peel. Cut into quarters and discard the core. Dice the apple, sprinkle with lemon juice and add to the salad bowl. Sprinkle on the sultanas and nuts. Add the mayonnaise and toss the salad well. Chill for a few minutes before serving.

AUSTRIAN LENTIL SALAD

SERVES 4–6
450 g (1 lb) lentils
1.8 litres (3 pints) water
2 bay-leaves
75 g (3 oz) onion
4 cloves
salt and pepper
¹/₂ teaspoon mustard powder
¹/₂ teaspoon paprika
6 spring onions
100 g (4 oz) dill pickled cucumbers
5 tablespoons olive oil
3 tablespoons red wine vinegar
3 tablespoons chopped fresh parsley

Preparation time: 10 minutes
Standing and cooking time: 4 ¹/₂ hours

Put the lentils in a bowl and cover with the water. Leave to stand for 4 hours. Put into a pan with the soaking water, bay-leaves, whole onion, cloves, salt and pepper. Cover and bring to the boil and then simmer until the lentils are tender but not mushy. Drain well and discard the bay-leaves and cloves and the onion.

Put into a bowl and mix with the mustard and paprika. Chop the spring onions and the cucumbers finely and sprinkle over the lentils. Mix the oil and vinegar, pour over the lentils and toss lightly. Sprinkle with a thick layer of parsley.

VENETIAN RICE SALAD

SERVES 4
225 g (8 oz) brown rice
600 ml (1 pint) vegetable stock
450 g (1 lb) shelled green peas
100 g (4 oz) vegetable margarine
25 g (1 oz) onion
1 teaspoon clear honey
pinch of ground nutmeg
salt and pepper
1 teaspoon chopped fresh tarragon or basil
4 tablespoons olive oil
1 tablespoon chopped fresh chives

Preparation time: 10 minutes
Cooking time: 20 minutes

Cook the rice in boiling salted water for 20 minutes until tender, adding a little water if necessary. Drain and put into a salad bowl to cool. While the rice is cooking, prepare the peas. If frozen peas are used, let them thaw first. Melt the margarine in a thick pan and add finely chopped onion, cooking over low heat until soft and golden, which will take about 5 minutes. Add the peas, honey, nutmeg, salt and pepper and 8 tablespoons water. Cover and cook very gently until the peas are tender but unbroken. Drain well and stir in the tarragon or basil. Leave until cold and then mix with the rice. Pour over the oil and toss lightly. Sprinkle with chives and serve at once.

PASTA NIÇOISE SALAD

SERVES 4
225 g (8 oz) pasta shells
4 hard-boiled eggs
4 large tomatoes
1 red pepper
100 g (4 oz) cooked French beans
8 black olives

1 teaspoon capers
4 tablespoons olive oil
2 tablespoons white wine vinegar
1 garlic clove
salt and pepper

Preparation time: 10 minutes
Cooking time: 12 minutes

Put the pasta into a large pan of boiling water and cook for 10–12 minutes until tender but unbroken. Drain very well, rinse in cold water and drain again. Place in a serving bowl. Cut the eggs in quarters lengthwise and quarter the tomatoes. Cut the peppers in half and discard the seeds and membranes. Slice the flesh thinly. Cut the beans into chunks. Mix the eggs, tomatoes, pepper and beans into the pasta and sprinkle with olives and capers. Mix the oil, vinegar, crushed garlic, salt and pepper and pour over the salad, tossing well before serving.

PRUNE AND APPLE SALAD

SERVES 4–6
350 g (12 oz) hard white cabbage
2 medium carrots
100 g (4 oz) cauliflower florets
2 celery sticks
2 eating apples
1 green or red pepper
100 g (4 oz) cucumbers
12 large prunes, soaked
150 ml (¹/₄ pint) mayonnaise
150 ml (¹/₂ pint) soured cream
salt and pepper
1 tablespoon chopped fresh chives

Preparation time: 15 minutes

Shred the cabbage finely and grate the carrots coarsely. Mix together in a serving bowl. Put the cauliflower florets into a pan of boiling salted water. Bring back to the boil and boil for 1 minute. Drain very well, rinse in cold water and pat dry with kitchen paper. Add to the cabbage and carrots. Chop the celery and peeled apples and add to the bowl. Cut the pepper in half, discard the seeds and membranes and slice the flesh thinly. Add to the bowl with the diced, peeled cucumber. Cut the prunes into small pieces with kitchen scissors and add to the bowl.

Beat together the mayonnaise, cream and plenty of salt and pepper. Pour over the salad and toss lightly. Sprinkle with chives and serve at once.

GOLDEN SALAD

SERVES 4
4 oranges
6 medium carrots
350 g (12 oz) cooked sweetcorn kernels
4 canned pineapple rings, in juice
4 canned apricot halves, in juice
1 lemon

Preparation time: 15 minutes

Peel the oranges and remove all white pith. Cut them across in thin slices and cut each slice in quarters. Grate the carrots coarsely and mix with the orange pieces in a bowl. If canned sweetcorn is used, drain very well and add to the bowl. If the sweetcorn is frozen, cook until just tender, drain very well and cool before adding to the bowl.

Drain the pineapple rings and apricot halves and chop roughly. Add to the bowl. Grate the lemon rind and squeeze out the juice. Add the rind and juice to the bowl, toss well and serve at once.

FRUIT SLAW

SERVES 4–6
450 g (1 lb) hard white cabbage
100 g (4 oz) black or white grapes
100 g (4 oz) slice of ripe melon
100 g (4 oz) black cherries
1 ripe peach
1 red-skinned eating apple
2 teaspoons lemon juice
300 ml (¹/₂ pint) soured cream
12 tablespoons clear honey
salt and pepper
1 tablespoon chopped fresh dill or fennel

Preparation time: 15 minutes

Shred the cabbage finely and place in a bowl. Cut the grapes in half and discard pips. Put the grapes in a second bowl with diced melon and stoned cherries. Peel the peach and dice the flesh and put onto a plate. Do not peel the apple but remove the core and dice the flesh. Mix with the peach and lemon juice. Just before serving, mix the cabbage and all the fruit. Mix the cream with the honey and plenty of salt and pepper. Pour over the salad and toss lightly. Sprinkle with chopped herbs and serve at once.

ORIENTAL SALAD

SERVES 4
450 g (1 lb) cottage cheese
6 tablespoons whipping cream
1 orange
250 g (1 oz) stem ginger
1 small crisp lettuce
1 bunch watercress
12 large black grapes

Preparation time: 15 minutes

Put the cottage cheese into a bowl. Whip the cream lightly and fold into the cheese. Peel the orange and divide into segments, skin each segment and chop the ginger finely. Stir the orange pieces and ginger into the cottage cheese mixture.

Wash and dry the lettuce and arrange a bed of lettuce on four serving plates. Discard large watercress stems and sprinkle the leaves and fine stems over the lettuce. Cut the grapes in half and discard the pips. Arrange the cottage cheese mixture in a heap on each bed of lettuce and watercress and garnish with grapes.

PLOUGHMAN'S SALAD

SERVES 4
150 ml (¹/₄ pint) olive oil
5 tablespoons cider vinegar
salt and pepper
2 toast-thickness slices day-old bread
100 g (4 oz) Cheddar or Edam cheese
100 g (4 oz) mozzarella cheese
4 tomatoes
¹/₄ cucumber
1 small crisp lettuce
6 spring onions

Preparation time: 15 minutes

Mix together the oil, vinegar and plenty of salt and pepper. Cut the bread into 1.25 cm (¹/₂ inch) cubes and add to the dressing. Toss the bread cubes so that they are coated lightly. Dice the cheeses and add to the bread. Skin the tomatoes and cut into eighths. Peel the cucumber and cut into small dice. Mix with the cheese and bread mixture. Wash and dry the lettuce and line a serving dish with lettuce leaves. Put the cheese and bread mixture into the centre with any dressing remaining in the bowl. Chop the spring onions finely and sprinkle over the surface.

BEETROOT IN SOURED CREAM

SERVES 4–6
450 g (1 lb) cooked beetroot
crisp lettuce leaves
300 ml (¹/₂ pint) soured cream
salt and pepper
2 tablespoons chopped fresh chives

Preparation time: 10 minutes

Cut the beetroot into small cubes or matchstick pieces. Arrange the lettuce leaves on a serving dish and pile the beetroot in the centre. Season the cream with plenty of salt and pepper and pour over the beetroot. Sprinkle with chives and chill before serving.

In the winter if the lettuce leaves are rather limp use chicory or Chinese cabbage as a base for the beetroot.

BROAD BEAN SALAD

SERVES 4
450 g (1 lb) cooked broad beans
3 tablespoons olive oil
1 tablespoon white wine vinegar
1 garlic clove
1 teaspoon French mustard
1 teaspoon paprika
salt and pepper
1 tablespoon chopped fresh summer savory or parsley

Preparation time: 10 minutes

If possible, use young tender beans for this salad. If older ones are used, slip then out of their skins while still hot, before adding the dressing. Put the beans into a bowl. Mix the oil and vinegar with crushed garlic, mustard, paprika, salt and pepper. Pour over the beans and toss well. Sprinkle with savory or parsley and serve at once. This salad is nicest if the beans are still slightly warm.

CRUNCHY CAULIFLOWER SALAD

SERVES 4–6
450 g (1 lb) cauliflower florets
1 small red pepper
12 pimento-stuffed green olives

50 g (2 oz) onion
4 tablespoons olive oil
2 tablespoons white wine vinegar
salt and pepper

Preparation time: 15 minutes

Cook the cauliflower in salted boiling water for 5 minutes and drain very well. Cool and put into a serving bowl. Cut the pepper in half and discard the seeds and membranes. Cut the pepper into thin strips and add to the cauliflower. Slice the olives thinly and chop the onion finely. Add to the bowl. Mix the oil, vinegar, salt and pepper. Pour over the salad, toss well and chill before serving.

GREEK CELERY SALAD

SERVES 4–6
1 medium head celery
300 ml (1/2 pint) vegetable stock
juice of 1 lemon
5 tablespoons olive oil
3 bay-leaves
15 g (1/2 oz) coriander seeds
salt and pepper
1 tablespoon chopped fresh parsley

Preparation time: 10 minutes
Cooking time: 15 minutes

Remove and discard the damaged outer stems from the celery, together with the leaves and root ends. Cut across into 5 cm (2 inch) lengths. Wash and dry very thoroughly, drain and put into a pan. Cover with boiling salted water and boil for 10 minutes. Drain very well and put into a clean saucepan. Add the vegetable stock, lemon juice, oil, bay-leaves, coriander, salt and pepper. Bring to the boil and them simmer until the celery pieces are tender and the liquid is thick and creamy. Put into a serving dish and leave until cold. Sprinkle with parsley just before serving.

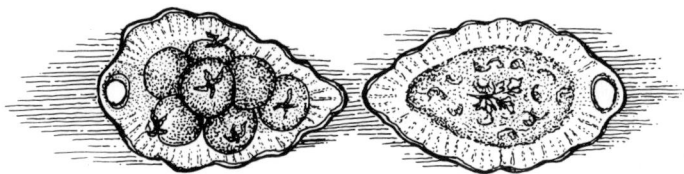

AUBERGINE AND TOMATO SALAD

SERVES 6
2 medium aubergines
5 large tomatoes
4 tablespoons olive oil
2 tablespoons lemon juice
salt and pepper
1 tablespoon chopped fresh basil or chives

Preparation time: 10 minutes
Cooking time: 20 minutes
Preheat the oven to 320°C/450°F/Gas mark 8.

Lightly oil a baking sheet. Wash and dry the aubergines but do not peel them. Put onto the baking sheet and bake for 20 minutes until the aubergine skins have burst. Remove the skins and put the pulp into a basin. Beat well until smooth. Skin the tomatoes and discard seeds. Chop the flesh roughly.

Spoon the aubergine pulp into a serving dish and top with chopped tomatoes. Mix the oil, lemon juice, salt and pepper and pour over the tomatoes. Chill before serving, and then toss well and sprinkle with chopped herbs.

FRENCH DRESSING

FOR 150 ML (¼ PINT) DRESSING
6 tablespoons olive, nut or salad oil
2 tablespoons wine vinegar or lemon juice
pinch of mustard powder
salt and pepper

Preparation time: 5 minutes

Put the ingredients into a screw-top jar and shake vigorously. Just before using, shake well again, as the oil floats to the surface. If liked, a pinch of sugar may be added, or some chopped mixed fresh herbs.

EASY MAYONNAISE

FOR 300 ML (½ PINT) MAYONNAISE
1 large egg
1 tablespoon wine vinegar or lemon juice
1 teaspoon sugar
½ teaspoon salt

¹/₄ teaspoon white pepper
¹/₄ teaspoon mustard powder
300 ml (¹/₂ pint) olive or salad oil

Preparation time: 10 minutes

Put the egg into a bowl with the lemon juice or vinegar, sugar, salt, pepper and mustard. Stir into a paste. Gradually add the oil, drop by drop, beating until the mixture is thick and creamy. Keep cool but do not chill.

This is a quick mayonnaise to make and not too rich. It is just about foolproof and the whole egg and oil amalgamate easily. If preparing a batch of mayonnaise in a blender or food processor, use this whole egg method rather than the traditional version with egg yolk only.

COOKED SALAD CREAM

FOR 900 ML (1 ¹/₂ PINTS) SALAD CREAM
100 g (4 oz) vegetable margarine
75 g (3 oz) plain flour
75 g (3 oz) sugar
15 g(1/2 oz) mustard powder
900 ml (1 ¹/₂ pints) milk
2 eggs
450 ml (³/₄ pint) white vinegar
salt and pepper

Preparation time: 20 minutes

Melt the margarine in a thick pan over low heat. Take off the heat and stir in the flour, sugar, mustard and enough milk to make a smooth paste. Return to low heat and stir gently, gradually adding the remaining milk. Cook until the sauce is thick and smooth. Take off the heat and beat well. Leave until luke-warm and beat in the eggs. Beat in the vinegar gradually, a little at a time, until the mixture is smooth and creamy. Season well with salt and pepper. Put into sterilized screw-top jars and store in a cool place for up to 6 weeks.

This is a traditional recipe which many people refer to mayonnaise as it is less rich, and the eggs are cooked.

YOGURT DRESSING

For 150 ml (¹/₄ pint) dressing
150 ml (¹/₄ pint) low fat natural yogurt
juice of ¹/₂ lemon
salt and pepper
1 tablespoon chopped fresh parsley

Preparation time: 5 minutes

Put the yogurt and lemon juice into a bowl and season well with salt and pepper. Add the parsley and stir well to mix. Serve in a jug or pour over salad just before serving. This is particularly good with tomatoes, cucumber and beetroot. Richer yogurt may be used if preferred, and for a salad which contains fruit, a tablespoon of honey and a little orange juice may be added.

EGGS AND CHEESE

Eggs and cheese are the mainstay of many vegetarian diets, but they need not just be served as a hard-boiled egg or lump of cheese as a meat substitute in family meals. Omelettes and pancakes with vegetable or cheese fillings are always delicious, and soufflés are remarkably easy to make and will impress family and guests. Dairy products may also be used for pâtés and spreads, for the fillings of flans and for enhancing pasta.

BAKED SPINACH WITH EGGS

SERVES 4
450 g (1 lb) fresh spinach
3 tablespoons olive oil
1 medium onion
8 eggs
salt and pepper
pinch of chopped basil
1 tablespoon chopped fresh parsley
50 g (2 oz) grated Parmesan cheese
2 large tomatoes
8 black olives

Preparation time: 10 minutes
Cooking time: 12 minutes
Preheat the oven to 180°C/350°F/Gas mark 4.

Use a shallow heavy pan which can be used on top of the stove and in the oven. Wash the spinach very throughly and remove the stems. Tear the leaves roughly. Heat the oil in the pan and cook the thinly sliced onion until soft and golden. Meanwhile, break the eggs into a large bowl and beat well. Add the salt, pepper, basil, parsley, cheese and spinach and mix together. Add to the onion slices in the pan and cook over low heat, lifting the mixture with a wide spatula so that the egg mixture runs through the spinach and begins to set. This will take about 3 minutes.

Slice the tomatoes thinly and arrange on top of the spinach. Stone the olives, chop roughly and sprinkle on top. Bake in the oven for 8 minutes and serve very hot. Any leftovers are good served very cold with crusty bread.

CARROT SOUFFLE

SERVES 4
450 g (1 lb) carrots
50 g (2 oz) onion
150 ml ($^1/_4$ pint) water
salt and pepper
25 g (1 oz) vegetable margarine
1 tablespoon plain flour
150 ml ($^1/_4$ pint) milk
4 eggs

Preparation time: 10 minutes
Cooking time: 1 $^1/_4$ hours
Preheat the oven to 180°C/350°F/Gas mark 4.

Scrape or peel the carrots and chop them roughly. Put into a pan with finely chopped onion, water and salt. Bring to the boil and then cover and simmer for about 20 minutes until the carrot pieces are soft. Drain well and mash thoroughly or blend into a purée with an electric blender or food processor. Season well with salt and pepper.

Melt the margarine in a thick pan. Add the flour and cook for 1 minute, stirring well. Take off the heat and gradually stir in the milk. Return to the heat and simmer until the sauce is thick and creamy, stirring well all the time. Mix into the carrot purée. Separate the eggs and beat the yolks into the carrot mixture. Whisk the egg whites to stiff peaks and fold into the carrots. Put into a greased 1.5 litre (2 $^1/_2$ pint) soufflé dish and bake for 45 minutes. Serve immediately.

CHEESE AND LEEK SOUFFLE

SERVES 4–6
50 g (2 oz) vegetable margarine
450g (1 1b) leeks
25g (1 oz) plain flour
150 ml ($^1/_4$ pint) milk
100 g (4 oz) grated Cheddar cheese
1 tablespoon grated Parmesan cheese
1 teaspoon made English mustard
salt and pepper
6 eggs

Preparation time: 10 minutes
Cooking time: 1 hour
Preheat the oven to 180°C/350°F/Gas mark 4.

Put half the margarine in a pan. Slice the leeks very thinly and put into the pan. Cook over low heat for about 8 minutes until the leeks are soft and well coated with the fat. Melt the remaining fat in another pan, work in the flour and cook for 1 minute. Remove from the heat and gradually stir in the milk. Cook for 1 minute and add the cheeses, mustard and plenty of salt and pepper. Remove from the heat, stir well and leave to cool for 5 minutes. Separate the eggs and beat the yolks into the cheese sauce. Drain the leeks very thoroughly and stir into the sauce.

Whisk the egg whites into stiff peaks and fold into the leek mixture. Place in a greased 1.2 litre (2 pint) soufflé dish and bake for 45 minutes. Serve immediately.

GARLIC CROUTON OMELETTE

SERVES 2
40 g (1 ¹/₂ oz) vegetable margarine
3 teaspoons oil
1 garlic clove
1 medium slice white bread
salt and pepper
3 eggs

Preparation time: 5 minutes
Cooking time: 10 minutes

The croûtons are made before preparing the omelette. Put 25g (1 oz) margarine and the oil into an omelette pan. Remove and discard the bread crusts and cut the bread into 1.25 cm (¹/₂ inch) cubes. Heat the margarine and oil and stir in the crushed garlic and bread cubes. Fry over high heat, tossing the pan, until the bread cubes are crisp and golden. Drain on kitchen paper and season well with salt and pepper.

Wipe the pan with a piece of kitchen paper and put in the remaining margarine. Beat the eggs with salt and pepper. Heat the pan and pour in the eggs. Cook for 2–3 minutes, moving the mixture with a fork so that the eggs are pushed from sides to middle of pan and the omelette becomes light and fluffy. Cook until the top is soft and still slightly runny but the base of the omelette is set and golden brown. Sprinkle the croûtons on the omelette and fold over. Tip onto a plate a cut in half. Serve at once with a green salad.

CHEESE SOUFFLE OMELETTE

SERVES 1
3 eggs
salt and pepper
15 g (¹/₂ oz) vegetable margarine
50 g (2 oz) grated Red Leicester cheese

Preparation time: 5 minutes
Cooking time: 5 minutes

Separate the eggs and beat the yolks with plenty of salt and pepper until creamy. Whisk the egg white to stiff peaks and fold into the yolks. Melt the margarine in an omelette pan and pour in the egg mixture. Cook over low heat until the base has set and is golden brown.

Carefully lift the omelette on to a warm flameproof plate. Sprinkle three-quarters of the cheese on top and fold in half. Sprinkle the remaining cheese on top. Put under a hot grill for 30 seconds to melt the cheese. Serve immediately.

ITALIAN RICOTTA PANCAKES

SERVES 4
100 g (4 oz) plain flour
pinch of salt
2 eggs
300 ml (¹/₂ pint) milk
2 teaspoons oil
oil for frying

Filling and Sauce:
225 g (8 oz) ricotta cheese
1 tablespoon grated Parmesan cheese
1 tablespoon chopped fresh marjoram
salt and pepper
25 g (1 oz) vegetable margarine
2 teaspoons plain flour
2 tablespoons tomato paste
150 ml (¹/₄ pint) vegetable stock

Preparation time: 10 minutes
Cooking time: 20 minutes

Prepare the pancakes first. Sieve the flour and salt into a bowl and beat in the eggs and a little milk. Beat to work in all the flour and gradually beat in the remaining milk and the oil. Heat a little oil in a 17.5 cm (7 inch) pancake pan. Pour in 2–3 tablespoons batter and tilt the pan so that the surface is covered. Cook over high heat for about 1 minute, turn and cook the other side for 30 seconds. Lift onto a plate and keep warm while cooking the rest of the batter to make 8 pancakes.

Put the ricotta cheese, Parmesan, marjoram, salt and pepper into a bowl and beat until creamy. Divide the filling between the pancakes and fold into quarters. Arrange in a single layer in a shallow flameproof dish.

Melt the margarine and stir in the flour. Cook for 1 minute and then stir in the tomato paste and stock, stirring well. Season with salt and pepper and simmer for 3 minutes, stirring all the time. Pour over the pancakes and put under a hot grill for 2 minutes before serving very hot.

BREAD AND CHEESE PANCAKES

SERVES 4
8 pancakes (see page 66)
1 medium slice white bread
50 g (2 oz) vegetable margarine
100g (4 oz) mozzarella cheese
salt and pepper
25 g (1 oz) grated Parmesan cheese

Preparation time: 5 minutes
Cooking time: 20 minutes

Prepare the pancakes (as in Italian Ricotta Pancakes) and keep warm. Remove and discard bread crusts and cut the bread into 1.25 cm ($^1/_2$ inch) cubes. Heat the margarine and cook the bread cubes until crisp and golden. Take off the heat. Cut the mozarella cheese into cubes and stir into the bread. Season well with salt and pepper. Divide the filling between the pancakes and roll up. Place in a single layer in a shallow flameproof dish. Sprinkle with Parmesan cheese and brown under a hot grill for 2 minutes until the cheese is bubbling. Serve at once with a tomato salad garnished with basil.

POTATO PANCAKES WITH RATATOUILLE

SERVES 2–3
2 large potatoes
50 g (2 oz) plain flour
2 eggs
175 ml (6 fluid oz) milk
salt and pepper
oil for frying
Ratatouille (see page 47)

Preparation time: 15 minutes
Cooking time: 15 minutes

Peel the potatoes and boil in salted water for 10 minutes until partly cooked. Drain well and grate coarsely into a bowl. Stir in the flour. Beat the eggs and milk together and work into the potatoes, beating well with a wooden spoon. Season well with salt and pepper.

Put a little oil into a heavy frying pan and heat until just smoking. Pour in about 4 tablespoons potato mixture and cook until golden on the base. Turn over and cook the other side until golden brown. Lift onto a warm serving plate and keep warm until all the potato mixture has been cooked. Serve topped with spoonfuls of hot Ratatouille (see page 47) or any other savoury topping preferred.

FARMHOUSE CHEESE PUDDING

SERVES 4
8 thin slices wholemeal bread
vegetable margarine for spreading
100 g (4 oz) grated Cheddar cheese
50 g (2 oz) grated Red Leicester cheese
3 eggs
450 g (³/₄ pint) milk
1 teaspoon made English mustard
1 tablespoon chopped fresh parsley
salt and pepper
2 tomatoes

Preparation time: 10 minutes
Standing and Cooking time: 1 ¹/₄ hours
Preheat the oven to 160°C/325°F/Gas mark 3.

Spread the bread with margarine and make into sandwiches with the Cheddar cheese. Cut off and discard the crusts. Cut each sandwich into triangles and arrange in two layers in a greased 1.2 litre (2 pint) pie dish. Sprinkle with Red Leicester cheese.

Beat the eggs and milk with the mustard, parsley and plenty of salt and pepper. Pour over the bread and leave to stand for 30 minutes. Bake for 30 minutes. Slice the tomatoes and arrange on top of the pudding. Continue baking for 45 minutes. Serve at once with a green salad.

CHEESE SOUFFLE FLAN

SERVES 6–8
350 g (12 oz) prepared shortcrust pastry (see page 86)
25 g (1 oz) plain flour
300 ml (¹/₂ pint) milk
100 g (4 oz) vegetable margarine

2 eggs
50 g (2 oz) grated Cheddar cheese
175 g (6 oz) Gruyère cheese
salt and pepper
pinch of ground nutmeg
pinch of mustard powder

Preparation time: 15 minutes
Cooking time: 1 hour
Preheat the oven to 200°C/400°F/Gas mark 6.

Line a 22.5 cm (9 inch) flan tin with pastry and chill for 10 minutes. Prick the pastry well with a fork and press a piece of foil into the tin. Bake for 15 minutes remove foil and leave to cool.

Mix the flour with a little of the milk and then gradually work in the remaining milk. Heat very gently, stirring well, until thick and creamy. Take off the heat. Cut the margarine into small pieces and stir into the sauce with the egg yolks and grated Cheddar cheese. Slice the Gruyère cheese thinly and arrange on the base of the flan case. Whisk the egg whites into soft peaks and fold into the sauce. Season well with salt, pepper, nutmeg and mustard. Pour into the pastry case, bake for 40 minutes and serve at once.

BRIE QUICHE

SERVES 6–8
350 g (12 oz) prepared shortcrust pastry (see page 86)
300 g (10 oz) ripe Brie cheese
1 egg and 1 egg white
50 g (2 oz) grated Gruyère cheese
salt and pepper
pinch of ground nutmeg

Preparation time: 15 minutes
Cooking time: 45 minutes
Preheat the oven to 200°C/400°F/Gas mark 6.

Line a 22.5cm (9 inch) flan tin with pastry and chill for 10 minutes. Prick the pastry well with a fork and press a piece of foil into the tin. Bake for 15 minutes, remove foil and leave to cool. Reduce oven heat to 180°C/350°F/Gas mark 4.

Break up the Brie and work with a fork until creamy. Gradually work in the egg, egg white and Gruyère cheese, and season well with salt, pepper and nutmeg. Spread in the pastry case and bake for 30 minutes. Serve hot.

NUTTY STILTON QUICHE

SERVES 6–8
350 g (12 oz) prepared shortcrust pastry (see page 86)
175 g (6oz) low fat cream cheese
100 g (4 oz) Stilton cheese
2 eggs
150 ml (¹/₄ pint) single cream
salt and pepper
100 g (4 oz) walnut kernels

Preparation time: 15 minutes
Cooking time: 45 minutes
Preheat the oven to 200°C/400°F/Gas mark 6.

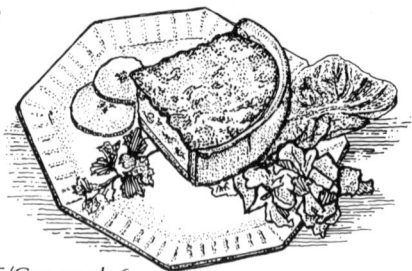

Line a 22.5 cm (9 inch) flan tin with pastry and chill for 10 minutes. Prick the pastry well with a fork and press a piece of foil into the tin. Bake for 15 minutes, remove foil, leave to cool.

Put the cream cheese and Stilton cheese into a bowl and mix lightly with a fork until they are broken up. Beat in the eggs and cream and season well with salt and pepper (taste carefully as the Stilton cheese might be slightly salty). Chop the walnuts roughly and sprinkle in the pastry case. Pour in the cheese mixture. Bake for 30 minutes. Serve hot.

WEST COUNTRY CHEESE FLAN

SERVES 6-8
350 g (12 oz) prepared shortcrust pastry (see page 86)
75 g (3 oz) onion
25 g (1 oz) vegetable margarine
1 large cooking apple
225 g (8 oz) grated Cheddar cheese
3 eggs
150 ml (¹/₄ pint) single cream
salt and pepper

Preparation time: 15 minutes
Cooking time: 45 minutes
Preheat the oven 200°C/400°F/Gas mark 6.

Line a 22.5 cm (9 inch) flan tin with pastry and chill for 10 minutes. Prick the pastry with a fork and press a piece of foil into the tin. Bake for 25 minutes, remove foil, leave to cool. Reduce oven heat to 190°C/375°F/Gas Mark 5.

Slice the onion thinly. Heat the margarine and cook the onion until soft over low heat. Sprinkle the cheese over the base of the pastry case.

Peel and core the apple and slice thinly. Arrange cooked onion and the apple slices over cheese. Beat together the eggs and cream and season well with salt and pepper. Pour into the pastry case and bake for 30 minutes. Serve hot or cold.

CHESTNUT FLAN

SERVES 6–8
350 g (12 oz) prepared shortcrust pastry (see page 86)
225 g (8 oz) unsweetened chestnut purée
50 g (2 oz) vegetable margarine
25 g (1 oz) plain flour
2 teaspoons French mustard
1 teaspoon chopped mixed fresh herbs
1 egg
150 ml (¹/₄ pint) creamy milk
50 g (2 oz) grated Cheddar cheese
salt and pepper
25 g (1 oz) fresh white or brown breadcrumbs
25 g (1oz) grated Parmesan cheese

Preparation time: 15 minutes
Cooking time: 45 minutes
Preheat the oven to 200°C/400°F/ Gas mark 6.

Line a 22.5 cm (9 inch) flan tin with pastry and chill for 10 minutes. Prick the pastry well with a fork and press a piece of foil into the tin. Bake for 15 minutes, remove the foil and leave to cool.

Put the chestnut purée into a pan with the margarine and heat to lukewarm. Stir in the flour, mustard and herbs and stir over low heat for 2 minutes. Take off the heat. Beat the egg and milk together and work into the mixture. Cook over low heat for 2 minutes. Take off the heat and stir in the Cheddar cheese and plenty of salt and pepper. Pour into the pastry case. Mix the breadcrumbs and Parmesan cheese and sprinkle onto the surface. Bake for 30 minutes. Serve hot.

FRESH HERB FLAN

SERVES 6–8
350 g (12 oz) prepared shortcrust pastry (see page 86)
50 g (2 oz) vegetable margarine
5 eggs
150 ml (¹/₄ pint) single cream
salt and pepper
2 tablespoons chopped fresh chives

1 tablespoon chopped fresh parsley
2 teaspoons chopped fresh thyme
2 teaspoons chopped fresh marjoram

Preparation time: 15 minutes
Cooking time: 25 minutes
Preheat the oven to 200°C/400°F/Gas mark 6.

Line a 22.5 cm (9 inch) flan tin with pastry and chill for 10 minutes. Prick the pastry well with a fork and press a piece of foil into the tin. Bake for 15 minutes and remove foil. Continue baking for 5 minutes.

While the pastry case is cooking, melt the margarine in a pan and stir in the lightly beaten eggs. Stir over low heat until just beginning to set. Take off the heat and stir in the cream. Season well with salt and pepper and stir in the herbs. Fill the pastry case and serve at once.

PROVENÇAL FLAN

SERVES 6
350 g (12 oz) prepared shortcrust pastry (see page 86)
450 g (1 lb) onions
6 tablespoons olive oil
2 garlic cloves
900 g (2 lb) tomatoes
sprig of thyme
1 bay-leaf
salt and pepper
6 eggs

Preparation time: 15 minutes
Cooking time: 1 hour
Preheat the oven to 200°C/400°F/Gas mark 6.

Line a 22.5 cm (9 inch) flan tin with pastry and chill for 10 minutes. Prick the pastry well with a fork and press a piece of foil into the tin. Bake for 15 minutes, remove foil and leave to cool.

While the pastry is cooking, chop the onions finely. Put into a pan with half the oil and the crushed garlic and cook over low heat for 15 minutes. Skin the tomatoes, discard the seeds and chop roughly. Put into another pan with the herbs and the remaining oil and simmer to a thick purée. Put the onions into the tomato purée. Mix well and season with salt and pepper. Discard the herbs. Spread the mixture in the pastry case and bake for 20 minutes. Just before serving, poach the eggs lightly. Remove the flan from the oven, arrange the eggs on top and serve at once.

MUSHROOM FLAN

SERVES 6–8
350 g (12 oz) prepared shortcrust pastry (see page 86)
450 g (1 lb) button mushrooms
juice of 1 lemon
40 g (1 ¹/₂ oz) vegetable margarine
15 g (¹/₂ oz) plain flour
150 ml (¹/₄ pint) milk
1 bay-leaf
sprig of thyme
150 ml (¹/₄ pint) double cream
2 egg yolks
salt and pepper

Preparation time: 15 minutes
Cooking time: 45 minutes
Preheat the oven to 200°C/400°F/ Gas mark 6.

Line a 22.5 cm (9 inch) flan tin with pastry and chill for 10 minutes. Prick the pastry well with a fork and press a piece of foil into the tin. Bake for 15 minutes, remove foil and leave to cool. Reduce oven heat to 190°C/375°F/Gas mark 5.

Do not peel the mushrooms but wipe them clean. Slice thinly and put into a pan with the lemon juice and margarine. Cook gently, tossing frequently, for 5 minutes. Stir in the flour and cook for 1 minute. Gradually add the milk and stir over low heat until smooth and thick. Add the bay-leaf and thyme, remove from the heat and leave until lukewarm. Discard the herbs. Stir in the cream and egg yolks and season well with salt and pepper. Spread in the pastry case. Bake for 30 minutes and serve hot.

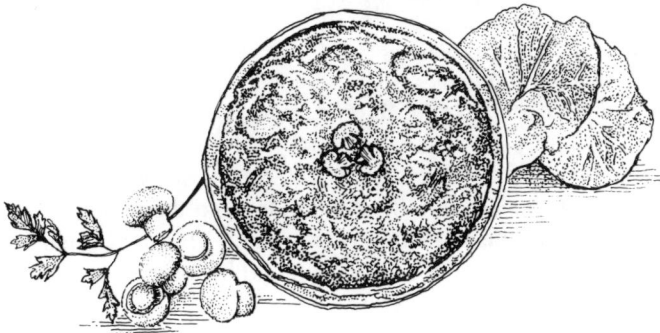

HOT AND COLD
PUDDINGS

There is no reason why a vegetarian pudding should be stodgy and dull, because all the traditional family favourites can be easily adapted so that everyone can enjoy them. Fresh fruit puddings, crumbles and charlottes, ices and steam puddings are all delicious fillers. Vegetarian suet, vegetable margarine and non-gelatine setting agents are easily bought, and the resulting dishes will be just as good as the traditional ones.

SPICED PEACHES

SERVES 4
4 large peaches
2 oranges
2 tablespoons redcurrant jelly
1 cinnamon stick
2 cloves
$^1/_2$ teaspoon whole allspice
50 g (2 oz) ground almonds
1 tablespoon finely chopped preserved ginger
1 tablespoon light soft brown sugar
2 tablespoons syrup from ginger

Preparation time: 10 minutes
Cooking time: 20 minutes
Preheat the oven to 180°C/350°F/Gas mark 4.

Do not peel the peaches but cut them in half downwards. Cut out the stones, making a small hole large enough to hold the filling, and reserve any cut flesh. Mix together the grated orange rind and juice with the redcurrant jelly and spices in a small pan and heat together until the jelly has melted.

Arrange the peaches cut side up in an ovenware dish. Mix together the ground almonds, chopped ginger, sugar and ginger syrup, and use the mixture to mix with any pieces of reserved peach flesh. Fill the cavities in the peaches. Bring the orange liquid to the boil and pour over the peaches. Bake for 20 minutes until the peaches are tender when pierced with a sharp knife. Serve hot or cold, with thick yogurt if liked.

WINTER FRUIT COMPOTE

SERVES 4
150 g (6 oz) dried apricots
450 ml (³/4 pint) dry cider
3 tablespoons clear honey
150 ml (¹/4 pint) water
1 cinnamon stick
2 cloves
50 g (2 oz) seedless raisins
1 grapefruit
2 bananas

Preparation time: 15 minutes
Soaking time: 2 hours
Cooking time: 30 minutes

Put the apricots into a bowl and cover them with cider. Leave to soak for 2 hours. Put into a pan with the honey, water, cinnamon stick and cloves. Bring to the boil and then simmer for about 25 minutes until the apricots are just soft. Add the raisins and continue simmering for 5 minutes.

While the fruit is cooking, peel the grapefruit and remove all the white pith. Divide between segments with a sharp knife so that the thin skin is removed and the pieces of fruit remain whole. Remove the pan from the heat and discard the cinnamon stick. Stir in the grapefruit segments. Peel the bananas and cut into chunks. Stir into the other fruit. Heat through gently until warm but not boiling. Serve warm, with cream or yogurt if liked.

CRUNCHY APRICOT CRUMBLE

SERVES 4
450 g (1 lb) fresh apricots
50 g (2 oz) caster sugar
50 g (2 oz) plain flour
¹/2 teaspoon baking powder
50 g (2 oz) porridge oats
75 g (3 oz) demerara sugar
50 g (2 oz) vegetable margarine
pinch of ground cinnamon

Preparation time: 10 minutes
Cooking time: 45 minutes
Preheat the oven to 200°C/400°F/Gas mark 6.

Cut the apricots in half and discard the stones. Place the apricots in an ovenware dish and sprinkle the caster sugar over the fruit. Stir together the flour, baking powder, oats and demerara sugar and rub in the margarine until the mixture is like coarse crumbs. Sprinkle in the ginger and mix well. Sprinkle over the fruit but do not press down. Bake for 45 minutes. Serve hot with cream.

BLACKBERRY AND APPLE SNOW

SERVES 4
450 g (1 lb) cooking apples
225 g (8 oz) blackberries
150 ml (¹/₄ pint) water
100 g (4 oz) caster sugar
juice of 1 lemon
150 ml (¹/₄ pint) double cream
2 egg whites

Preparation time: 15 minutes
Cooking time: 15 minutes

Use the type of apple which becomes light and fluffy when cooked. Peel and core the apples and slice them thinly into a pan. Add the blackberries, water and 75 g (3 oz) sugar. Cover and simmer for 15 minutes. Cool slightly and put through a sieve. Leave until cold and stir in the lemon juice and the cream. Whisk the egg whites to stiff peaks and fold in the remaining sugar. Fold this mixture into the fruit purée. Put into a serving dish or individual glasses and chill before serving.

BLACKCURRANT LINZER TORTE

SERVES 6
225 g (8 oz) plain flour
1 teaspoon ground cinnamon
150 g (5 oz) block margarine
40 g (1 ¹/₂ oz) ground almonds
40 g (1 ¹/₂ oz) caster sugar
1 egg
1 ¹/₂ teaspoons lemon juice
675 g (1 ¹/₂ lb) blackcurrants
175 g (6 oz) granulated sugar
sugar for sprinkling

Preparation time: 15 minutes
Cooking time: 30 minutes
Preheat the oven to 200°C/400°F/Gas mark 6.

Stir the flour and cinnamon together and rub in the margarine until the mixture is like fine breadcrumbs. Stir in the almonds and caster sugar and make into a dough with the egg and lemon juice. Roll out carefully and line a 20 cm (8 inch) flan tin, reserving any surplus pastry for decoration.

Remove any stems from fruit and place the fruit in the pastry case, sprinkling with sugar. Roll out the surplus pastry and cut into 1.25 cm (1/2 inch) strips. Arrange in a lattice on top of the fruit. Brush the lattice with water and sprinkle with sugar. Bake for 30 minutes and serve hot or cold.

RASPBERRY CRUMB PUDDING

SERVES 4
450 g (1 lb) raspberries
100 g (4 oz) caster sugar
25 g (1 oz) vegetable margarine
100 g (4 oz) fresh white breadcrumbs
3 eggs

Preparation time 10 minutes
Standing and cooking time: 1 1/2 hours
Chilling time: 3 hours

Put the raspberries into a pan with the sugar and heat gently until the juice runs. Put the fruit and juice through a sieve and return to the pan. Heat gently with the margarine and pour over the breadcrumbs. Leave to stand for 30 minutes.

Preheat the oven to 180°C/350°F/Gas mark 4. Beat the eggs and mix with the raspberry soaked crumbs. Put into a lightly greased ovenware bowl and bake for 1 hour. Cool completely then chill in the refrigerator for 3 hours. Turn on to a serving plate and dust with a little sieved icing sugar. Serve with cream.

RHUBARB BETTY

SERVES 4–6
675 g (1 1/2 lb) rhubarb
100 g (4 oz) sugar
1 orange
225 g (8 oz) soft white breadcrumbs
75 (3 oz) shredded vegetable suet

Preparation time: 15 minutes
Cooking time: 1 hour 10 minutes
Preheat the oven to 180°C/350°F/Gas mark 4.

Cut the rhubarb into small pieces and put into a pan with the sugar. Grate the orange rind and squeeze out the juice. Add the rind and the juice to the rhubarb, with just enough water to cover. Simmer until the fruit is tender.

Mix the breadcrumbs and suet together. Grease an ovenware dish and put in a 2.5 cm (1 inch) layer of the crumb mixture. Bake for 10 minutes. Remove from the oven and put in alternate layers of rhubarb and crumbs, ending with crumbs. Bake for 1 hour. Serve hot or cold with cream or custard.

SUMMER FRUIT BOWL

SERVES 4
225 g (8 oz) strawberries
225 g (8 oz) raspberries
100 g (4 oz) blackcurrants
100g (4 oz) redcurrants
100 g (4 oz) black cherries
175 g (6 oz) caster sugar
2 tablespoons cassis or kirsch (optional)

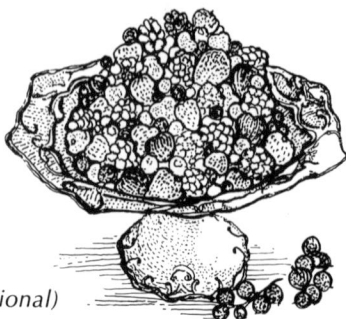

Preparation time: 10 minutes
Chilling time: 2 hours

Hull the strawberries and place in a serving bowl, sprinkling with a little sugar. Add the raspberries and a little more sugar. Remove stems from currants and add to the bowl with more sugar. Stone the cherries and add the fruit to the bowl with the remaining sugar. Toss the fruit lightly with a large spoon, adding the cassis or kirsch if liked. Cover and chill for 2 hours. Serve with cream.

AUTUMN PUDDING

SERVES 4–6
350 g (12 oz) blackberries
225 g (8 oz) cooking apples
300 ml (¹/₂ pint) cooking cider
175 g (6 oz) sugar
5 slices white or wholemeal bread from a large loaf

Preparation time: 15 minutes
Chilling time: 24 hours

Put the blackberries into a pan. Peel and core the apples into thin slices. Add the cider and sugar and simmer until the fruit is soft. Cool to lukewarm. Line a lightly oiled pudding basin with four bread slices, overlapping them, and making sure that the base and the sides of the bowl are covered. Pour in the fruit and juices and top with the remaining bread. Stand the bowl in a deep soup plate or dish. Put a plate on top of the bowl and heavy weights on top of the plate. Leave in a cold place for 24 hours. Turn onto a serving dish and spoon over any juices which have run out. Serve with cream.

BLACKCURRANT SHORTCAKE

SERVES 6
450 g (1 lb) blackcurrants
100 g (4 oz) granulated sugar
100 g (4 oz) vegetable margarine
100 g (4 oz) caster sugar
2 eggs
100 g (4 oz) self-raising flour
pinch of salt
300 ml (1/2 pint) double cream

Preparation time: 20 minutes
Cooking time: 25 minutes
Preheat the oven to 190°C/375°F/Gas mark 5.

Remove stems from currants, and put the fruit into a pan with the granulated sugar and 4 tablespoons water. Simmer until the fruit is tender then cool completely. While the fruit is cooling, cream together the margarine and caster sugar until light and fluffy. Beat in the eggs, one at a time, alternately with the flour. Add the salt and beat well. Put into two greased 17.5 cm (7 inch) sandwich tins. Bake for 25 minutes and turn onto a wire rack to cool.

Whip the cream to soft peaks. Place one shortcake on a serving dish and top with the blackcurrants. Put on the whipped cream and top with the second shortcake. Dust the top with a little sieved icing sugar and serve at once.

PLUM COBBLER

SERVES 4–6
450 g (1 lb) Victoria plums
3 oranges
3 tablespoons clear honey
225 g (8 oz) wholemeal flour
2 teaspoons baking powder
1 teaspoon ground mixed spice
1/2 teaspoon salt
25 g (1 oz) vegetable margarine
25 g (1 oz) light soft brown sugar
150 ml (1/4 pint) natural yogurt
beaten egg to glaze

Preparation time: 15 minutes
Baking time: 15 minutes
Preheat the oven to 220°C/425°F/Gas mark 7.

Cut the plums in half and discard the stones. Place the plums in a baking dish. Squeeze the juice from 2 oranges and add to the plums.

Grate the rind from the last orange and keep on one side. Peel the orange, remove all pith, and divide the orange into segments. Mix with the plums and spoon the honey over the fruit.

Put the flour, baking powder, spice and salt in a bowl and mix thoroughly until evenly coloured. Rub in the margarine until the mixture is like coarse breadcrumbs. Stir in the sugar and reserve orange rind. Mix in the yogurt to make a soft dough. Roll out on a lightly floured surface to about 1.25 cm (¹/₂ inch) thick and cut into 8–10 circles with a biscuit cutter. Arrange overlapping round the edge of the dish and brush with beaten egg. Bake for 15 minutes. Serve hot with custard or cream.

RASPBERRY YOGURT ICE

SERVES 4–6
450 g (1 lb) raspberries
150 ml (¹/₄ pint) double cream
150 ml (¹/₄ pint) natural yogurt
175 g (6oz) clear honey
2 tablespoons lemon juice
pinch of salt
4 egg whites

Preparation time: 10 minutes
Freezing time: 3 hours

Sieve the raspberries and discard the pips. Whip the cream to soft peaks and mix with the yogurt, honey, lemon juice, salt and raspberry purée. Stir together until evenly coloured. Put into a freezer container and freeze in the ice-making compartment of the refrigerator at lowest setting (or in the freezer) for 1 hour until the mixture looks like slightly thawed snow. Scoop into a cold bowl and beat until soft. Whisk the egg whites to stiff peaks and fold into the fruit mixture. Return to the freezer container and continue freezing for 2 hours.

HONEY PUDDING WITH LEMON SAUCE

SERVES 4–6
50 g (2 oz) clear honey
50 g (2 oz) vegetable margarine
1 egg
175 g (6 oz) plain flour
1 teaspoon baking powder
pinch of salt
3–4 tablespoons milk
50 g (2 oz) seedless raisins
grated rind of 1 lemon

Sauce:
50 g (2 oz) clear honey
150 ml (¹/₄ pint) water
juice of 1 lemon
2 teaspoons cornflour

Preparation time: 10 minutes
Cooking time: 1 ¹/₂ hours

Cream together the honey and margarine and beat in the egg. Sieve the flour with the baking powder and salt and work into the creamed mixture. Add a little milk to make a soft dropping consistency. Stir in the raisins and lemon rind. Grease a 600 ml (1 pint) pudding basin and put in the mixture. Cover with greaseproof paper and a piece of foil and tie securely with string. Put into a pan of boiling water (or into a steamer) and cook for 1 ¹/₂ hours, adding a little more boiling water if necessary to prevent drying-out.

Just before serving, mix all the sauce ingredients together, bring to the boil and simmer for 3 minutes. Turn the pudding onto a warm serving plate, and pour over a little sauce. Serve the rest separately.

STAWBERRY MALAKOFF

SERVES 6
18 sponge fingers
2 oranges
2 tablespoons sweet sherry
100 g (4 oz) vegetable margarine
100 g (4 oz) light soft brown sugar
225 g (8 oz) curd cheese
175 g (6 oz) ground almonds
450 g (1 lb) strawberries

Preparation time: 20 minutes
Chilling time: 4 hours

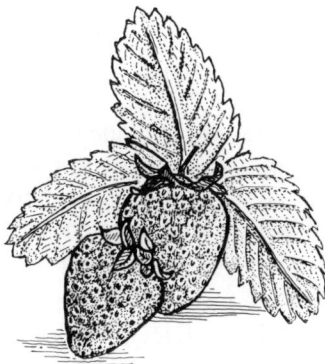

Line the base of a 15 cm (6 inch) round cake tin with non-stick parchment paper. Trim one end from each sponge finger so that they fit the depth of the tin. Reserve the trimmings. Grate the rind from the oranges and keep on one side. Squeeze out the juice and mix with the sherry. Dip in the sponge fingers one at a time, and arrange with rounded side down, round the edge of the tin. Save any surplus liquid.

Cream the margarine and sugar until light and fluffy. Add curd cheese, almonds, orange rind and reserved liquid and beat well. Hull the strawberries and keep one-third of them in reserve. Slice the rest thinly. Put one-third of the almond cream in the base of the tin. Cover with half the sliced berries and the reserved sponge trimmings. Cover this with one-third almond mixture and the remaining sliced berries and sliced trimmings. Top with the remaining almond mixture and level the surface. Cover with a plate and a weight and chill for 4 hours. Turn out on a serving plate and decorate with whole stawberries.

APRICOT SYLLABUB

SERVES 6
225 g (8 oz) dried apricots
600 ml (1 pint) water
1 lemon
150 ml (^{1}/4 pint) natural yogurt
2 tablespoons orange liqueur
50 g (2 oz) light soft brown sugar
2 egg whites
chopped nuts to decorate

Preparation time: 15 minutes
Soaking time: overnight
Cooking time: 30 minutes

Cover the apricots with the water. Grate the lemon rind and squeeze out the juice. Add rind and juice to the apricots and leave to soak overnight. Tip apricots and liquid into a pan. Blend in a liquidizer or food processor until smooth. Put into a bowl and leave until cold.

Add the yogurt, liqueur and sugar to the apricot purée and stir well until thoroughly mixed. Whisk the egg whites to soft peaks and fold into the mixture. Spoon into individual glasses and chill before serving. Sprinkle with chopped nuts just before serving.

SWEET CARROT PUDDING

SERVES 6–8
675 g (1 ^{1}/2 lb) carrots
225 g (8 oz) fine breadcrumbs
175 g (6 oz) vegetable suet
100 g (4 oz) currants
100 g (4 oz) seedless raisins
100 g (4 oz) soft brown sugar
pinch of salt
pinch of ground nutmeg
3 eggs
300 ml (^{1}/2 pint) milk

Preparation time: 30 minutes
Cooking time: 1 1/2 hours
Preheat the oven to 180°C/350°F/Gas mark 4.

Scrape the carrots and boil in lightly salted water until tender. Either sieve or blend in a liquidizer or food processor. Mix the carrot purée with breadcrumbs, suet, currants, raisins, sugar, salt and nutmeg. Beat in the eggs and enough milk to make a stiff batter. Put into a greased ovenware dish and bake for 1 1/2 hours. Serve hot with cream or custard.

TREACLE CREAM TART

SERVES 6
225 g (8 oz) prepared shortcrust pastry (see page 86)
225 g (8 oz) golden syrup
50 g (2 oz) vegetable margarine
1 egg
5 tablespoons single cream
1/2 teaspoon grated lemon rind

Preparation time: 15 minutes
Cooking time: 30 minutes
Preheat the oven to 200°C/400°F/Gas mark 6.

Line a 20 cm (8 inch) flan tin with the pastry. Heat the syrup very gently with the margarine until the fat has melted. Remove from the heat and stir in the egg and cream with the lemon rind. Pour into the pastry case and bake for 30 minutes. Serve hot or cold.

BAKED HONEY CHEESECAKE

SERVES 6
225 g (8 oz) prepared shortcrust pastry (see page 86)
225 g (8 oz) cottage cheese
100 g (4 oz) clear honey
100 g (4 oz) caster sugar
grated rind 1/2 lemon
75 g (3 oz) sultanas
4 eggs
pinch of ground cinnamon
sieved icing sugar

Preparation time: 15 minutes
Cooking time: 45 minutes

Preheat the oven to 200°C/400°F/Gas mark 6. Line a 20 cm (8 inch) flan tin with the pastry and chill for 10 minutes. Prick the pastry well with a fork and press a piece of foil into the tin. Bake for 15 minutes, remove foil and leave to cool. Reduce oven heat to 190°C/375°F/Gas mark 5.

Sieve the cottage cheese and stir into the honey, sugar, lemon rind and sultanas. Beat the eggs lightly and then beat them into the honey with a pinch of cinnamon. Pour into the pastry case and bake for 30 minutes. Cool to lukewarm. Serve warm, dusted lightly with icing sugar mixed with a little cinnamon.

LEMON TART

SERVES 6
225 g (8 oz), prepared shortcrust pastry (see page 86)
2 eggs
200 g (7 oz) caster sugar
75 g (3 oz) vegetable margarine
2 lemons

Preparation time: 15 minutes
Cooking time: 35 minutes
Preheat the oven to 190°C/375°F/Gas mark 5.

Line a 20 cm (8 inch) flan tin with the pastry. Beat together the eggs and the sugar. Soften the margarine and gradually beat into the egg mixture. Grate the rind and squeeze juice from the lemons. Add to the egg mixture and pour into the pastry case. Bake for 35 minutes. Leave until cold before serving.

CARAMELIZED APPLE TART

SERVES 6
75 g (3 oz) vegatable margarine
150 g (5oz) granulated sugar
5 eating apples
225 g (8 oz) prepared shortcrust pastry (see page 86)

Preparation time: 20 minutes
Cooking time: 25 minutes
Preheat the oven to 220°C/425°F/Gas mark 7.

Grease a 20 cm (8 inch) flan tin thickly on the bottom and the sides with 50 g (2 oz) margarine. Sprinkle with 50 g (2 oz) sugar. Peel and core the apples and slice thinly. Arrange a layer of apples on the sugar and sprinkle with 50 g (2 oz) sugar. Top with the remining apple slices. Cover with the pastry, tucking it in lightly round the apples with the tips of the fingers.

Bake for 20 minutes, and remove from the oven. Increase oven heat to 230°C/450°F/Gas mark 8. Turn the flan onto an ovenware flat plate and sprinkle with the remaining sugar. Cut the remaining margarine into thin flakes and sprinkle on top. Bake for 5 minutes. Serve with warm cream.

CHRISTMAS PUDDING

MAKES 4 PUDDINGS
225 g (8 oz) self-raising flour
225 g (8 oz) fresh breadcrumbs
225 g (8 oz) vegetarian suet
225 g (8 oz) currants
225 g (8 oz) dark soft brown sugar
350 g (12 oz) sultanas
350 g (12 oz) stoned raisins
1 orange
1 lemon
100 g (4 oz) glacé cherries
100 g (4 oz) chopped mixed candied peel
6 eggs
1 teaspoon salt
1 teaspoon ground mixed spice
300 ml ($^1/_2$ pint) brown ale
1 small carrot
1 small eating apple

Preparation time: 20 minutes
Cooking time: 8 hours

In a large bowl, mix the flour, breadcrumbs, suet, currants, sugar, sultanas and raisins. Grate the rind and squeeze the juice from the orange and lemon and add to the bowl. Chop the cherries and add to the bowl with the peel. Beat the eggs well and add to the mixture with the salt, spice and ale. Peel the carrot and apple and grate into the bowl. Stir thoroughly to make a stiff mixture. Grease four 900 ml (1 $^1/_2$ pint) bowls and put a small circle of greaseproof paper in the base of each one. Divide the mixture between them, and cover with greased greaseproof paper and foil, tying firmly with string. Put each bowl into a pan of boiling water to come halfway up the bowl (or into a steamer), cover and cook gently for 8 hours, topping up with boiling water from time to time so that the pan does not boil dry.

Remove puddings from the pan, take off wrappings and leave until cold. Put on clean dry greaseproof paper and foil and tie tightly with string. Either store in a cool dry place, or in the freezer. When serving, boil for 3 hours and turn out to serve with custard, cream or brandy butter.

HEALTHY BAKING

B read, pastry, cakes and biscuits are always a treat, although sweet things should really only be indulged in on special occasions, at weekends or when guests are entertained. Home-baked cakes and biscuits also provide useful fillers for lunch-boxes, or emergency sweet courses for main meals. They are extra delicious when made with honey, natural sugars and plenty of dried fruits, or with the addition of home-made jam.

SHORTCRUST PASTRY (WHOLEWHEAT)

MAKES 350 G (12 OZ) PREPARED PASTRY
225 g (8 oz) wholewheat flour
pinch of salt
100 g (4 oz) vegetable margarine
2 egg yolks
1 tablespoon iced water

Preparation time: 10 minutes

Stir the flour and salt together in a bowl and rub in the margarine until the mixture is like fine breadcrumbs. Beat the egg yolks and water and work into the flour to make a dough. Knead very lightly for one minute to mix well.

This pastry is a little fragile and it is a good idea to roll it out on a piece of lightly floured kitchen foil so that it can be lifted out into a tin. For a sweet pastry, add 25 g (1 oz) light soft brown sugar to the flour before mixing with the liquid.

This pastry is suitable for all the recipes in this book. Any surplus may be used for jam tarts or small savoury flans. The egg yolks give a crisper pastry than is usual with wholemeal flour, but a mixture of brown and white flours may be used for a lighter result. It is important to use hard block margarine or other fat, and not the soft creamed variety which is used for cakes.

BROWN SODA BREAD

MAKES ONE 17.5 CM (7 INCH) LOAF
350 g (12 oz) wholemeal bread flour
100 g (4 oz) white bread flour
1 teaspoon sea salt
1 teaspoon light soft brown sugar
2 teaspoons cream of tartar
1 teaspoon bicarbonate of soda
15 g ($^1/_2$ oz) vegetable margarine
300 ml ($^1/_2$ pint) milk

Preparation time: 15 minutes
Baking time: 35 minutes
Preheat the oven to 200°C/400°F/Gas mark 6.

Stir the flours, salt, sugar, cream of tartar and soda together. Rub in the margarine and mix with the milk to a soft dough. Turn onto a lightly floured board and knead lightly until smooth. Shape into a 17.5 cm (7 inch) circle and put onto a floured baking sheet. Brush with a little extra milk and cut a deep cross on top from side to side with a sharp knife. Bake for 40 minutes. Cool on a wire rack and serve freshly baked. This is an easy and delicious loaf which is quick to make, and is useful when yeast is not available.

FARMHOUSE BREAD

MAKES FOUR 450 G (1 LB) LOAVES
1.35 kg (3 lb) wholemeal bread flour
20 g ($^3/_4$ oz) sea salt
25 g (1 oz) vegetable margarine
25 g (1 oz) fresh yeast or 15 g ($^1/_2$ oz) dried yeast
900 ml (1 $^1/_2$ pints) lukewarm water

Preparation time: 15 minutes
Standing time: 1 hour
Cooking time: 35 minutes

Stir the flour and salt together in a warm bowl and rub in the margarine. Sprinkle the yeast on the water and leave for a few minutes until bubbling vigorously. Mix into the flour to form a soft but not sticky dough. Turn onto a lightly floured board and knead for 5 minutes until smooth. Put into a lightly greased warm bowl, cover with a cloth and leave in a warm place for 35 minutes until doubled in size.

Preheat the oven to 230°C/450°F/Gas mark 8. Turn the dough onto a lightly floured board and knead again for 5 minutes. Cut into four pieces (do not tear the dough which will spoil the rising of the bread). Shape each piece to fit a greased 450 g (1 lb) loaf tin. Cover with a cloth and leave in a warm place for about 25 minutes until the dough has just risen above the rim of the tins. Bake for 20 minutes. Reduce oven heat to 220°C/425°F/Gas mark 7 and continue baking for 15 minutes. Cool on a wire rack.

CHEESE LOAF

MAKES 1 450 G (1 LB) LOAF
225 g (8 oz) wholemeal bread flour
1 teaspoon sea salt
1 teaspoon English mustard powder
100 g (4 oz) Cheddar cheese
15 g ($^1/_2$ oz) fresh yeast or 7 g ($^1/_4$ oz) dried yeast
150 ml ($^1/_4$ pint) lukewarm water

Preparation time: 15 minutes
Standing time: 1 hour 20 minutes
Baking time: 45 minutes

Put the flour, salt, mustard powder and cheese into a warm bowl and stir well to mix. Sprinkle the yeast onto the water and leave to stand for a few minutes until frothing vigorously. Mix into the flour to make a soft dough (flours vary in absorbency and a little more water may be needed but the dough should not be sticky). Turn onto a lightly floured surface and knead for 5 minutes until smooth. Put the ball of dough into a greased warm bowl. Cover and leave in a warm place for an hour until doubled in size.

Preheat the oven to 220°C/425°F/Gas mark 7. Turn the dough onto a lightly floured surface and knead again for 3 minutes. Fold in three and place in a greased 450 g (1 lb) loaf tin, seam downwards. Cover with a cloth and leave in a warm place for about 20 minutes until the dough has risen to the top of the tin. Bake for 10 minutes. Reduce oven heat to 190°C/375°F/Gas mark 5 and continue baking for 35 minutes. Cool on a wire rack. Serve freshly baked.

COTTAGE CHEESE DROP SCONES

MAKES 10–12
225 g (1 oz) vegetable margarine
100 g (4 oz) cottage cheese
2 eggs
50 g (2 oz) white or wholemeal self-raising flour
1 tablespoon milk
oil for greasing

Preparation time: 10 minutes
Cooking time: 10 minutes

Melt the margarine and add to the cottage cheese. Mix well then beat in the eggs, flour and milk to make a smooth thick batter. Heat a griddle or heavy frying pan and grease lightly with a little oil. Drop tablespoonsful of batter onto the hot surface. Cook for 1 minute until just set. Turn with a palette knife and continue cooking for 1 minute. Turn again and continue cooking until the griddlecakes are set and golden.

Lift onto a wire rack and cover with a clean cloth to keep warm and soft while the rest of the batter is cooked. Serve at once with a savoury spread or honey. These scones are particularly good for those who enjoy the flavour of home-baking but do not want to eat a lot of flour or sugar.

YOGURT SCONES

MAKES 12–15
225 g (8 oz) plain white or wholemeal flour
$^1/_2$ teaspoon of salt
1 $^1/_2$ teaspoons baking powder
25 g (1 oz) vegetable margarine
150 ml ($^1/_4$ pint) natural yogurt

Preparation time: 15 minutes
Cooking time: 12 minutes
Preheat the oven to 200°C/400°F/Gas mark 6.

Stir together the flour, salt and baking powder. Rub in the fat until the mixture is like fine breadcrumbs. Mix in the yogurt to give a soft but not sticky dough. Knead very lightly until smooth. Roll out 2 cm ($^3/_4$ inch) thick. Cut into 5 cm (2 inch) rounds. Put onto a lightly floured baking sheet so that the scones just touch each other. Bake for 12 minutes. Cool on a wire rack. Serve freshly baked, split and spread with margarine or butter, or with jam and cream.

HONEY BRAN MUFFINS

MAKES 18
100 g (4 oz) plain flour
2 teaspoons baking powder
$^1/_3$ teaspoon salt
40 g (1 $^1/_2$ oz) vegetable margarine
50 g (2 oz) bran cereal
50 g (2 oz) chopped mixed nuts
1 egg
8 tablespoons clear honey
7 tablespoons milk

Preparation time: 10 minutes
Cooking time: 20 minutes
Preheat the oven to 220°C/425°F/Gas mark 5.

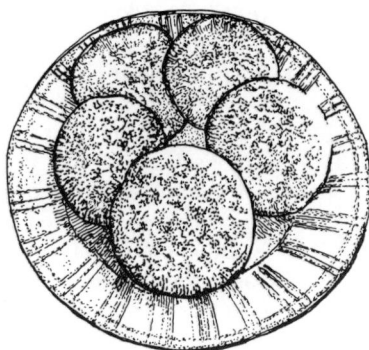

Sieve together the flour, baking powder and salt. Rub in the margarine until the mixture is like coarse breadcrumbs. Stir in the cereals and nuts. Beat the egg, honey and milk together, and beat in the dry ingredients. Grease 18 deep patty tins and divide the mixture between them. Bake for 20 minutes. Serve freshly baked and still slightly warm, spread with margarine or butter.

HONEY DATE BARS

MAKES 16
100 g (4 oz) clear honey
75 g (3 oz) vegetable margarine
1 teaspoon vanilla essence
3 eggs
175 g (6 oz) plain flour
1 teaspoon baking powder
¹/₂ teaspoon salt
175 g (6 oz) chopped dates
100 g (4 oz) chopped mixed nuts

Preparation time: 10 minutes
Cooking time: 30 minutes
Preheat the oven to 180°C/375°F/Gas mark 5.

Put the honey, margarine and essence into a bowl and beat until light and creamy. Beat the eggs lightly together. Sieve the flour with the baking powder and salt. Add eggs and flour alternately to the creamed mixture. Stir in the dates and nuts. Grease a 30 x 23 cm (12 x 9 inch) baking tin and spread on the mixture. Bake for 30 minutes. Cool in the tin and then cut into bars and lift out carefully. Just before serving, sprinkle with a little sieved icing sugar.

HONEY GINGERBREAD LOAF

MAKES ONE 450 G (1 LB) LOAF
50 g (2 oz) vegetable margarine
150 g (5 oz) clear honey
150 g (5 oz) demerara sugar
300 g (10 oz) plain flour
pinch of salt
1 teaspoon bicarbonate of soda
1 teaspoon ground mixed spice
1 teaspoon ground cinnamon
2 teaspoons ground ginger
100 g (4 oz) chopped mixed candied peel
1 egg
150 ml (¹/₄ pint) milk
25 g (1 oz) flaked almonds

Preparation time: 10 minutes
Cooking time: 1 ¹/₄ hours
Preheat the oven to 180°C/350°F/Gas mark 4.

Grease and line the base of a 450 g (1 lb) loaf tin with greaseproof paper. Put the margarine into a pan and heat gently until melted. Remove from the heat and stir in the honey and sugar until well mixed. Cool to lukewarm. Sieve together the flour, salt, soda and spices, and stir in the peel. Beat the egg and milk lightly together and stir into the honey mixture. Make a well in the centre of the dry ingredients and pour in the liquid, beating well until smooth. Pour into the prepared tin and sprinkle almonds on the surface. Bake for 1 ¹/₄ hours. Cool in the tin for 5 minutes and turn onto a wire rack to cool. Serve sliced and spread with margarine or butter.

YOGURT SPICE CAKE

MAKES ONE 17.5 CM (7 INCH) SQUARE CAKE
100 g (4 oz) vegetable margarine
50 g (2 oz) light soft brown sugar
50 g (2 oz) black treacle
175 g (6 oz) golden syrup
150 ml (¹/₄ pint) natural yogurt
2 eggs
225 g (8 oz) plain flour
3 teaspoons ground ginger
1 teaspoon ground mixed spice
¹/₄ teaspoon bicarbonate of soda

Preparation time: 15 minutes
Cooking time: 1 ¹/₄ hours
Preheat the oven to 150°C/350°F/Gas mark 2.

Grease and line the base of a 17.5 cm (7 inch) square cake tin with greaseproof paper. Put the margarine, sugar, treacle and syrup into a pan and heat gently until the fat has melted and the sugar dissolved. Cool to lukewarm. Beat the yogurt and eggs together lightly and stir into the mixture. Stir together the flour, ginger, spice and soda and beat in the liquid. Put into the tin and bake for 1 ¹/₂ hours. Cool in the tin for 10 minutes and turn onto a wire rack to cool. If possible, store in an airtight tin for 24 hours before cutting.

CARROT CAKE WITH CREAM CHEESE ICING

MAKES ONE 20 CM (8 INCH) ROUND CAKE
350 g (12 oz) carrots
225 g (8 oz) vegetable margarine
225 g (8 oz) light soft brown sugar
4 eggs
1 tablespoon lemon juice
2 teaspoons grated orange rind
225 g (8 oz) self-raising flour
100 g (4 oz) chopped walnuts

Icing:
225 g (8 oz) cream cheese
1 tablespoon clear honey
2 teaspoons lemon juice
8 walnut halves

Preparation time: 15 minutes
Cooking time: 1 ¹/₂ hours
Preheat the oven to 180°C/350°F/Gas mark 4.

Grease and line the base of a 20 cm (8 inch) round cake tin with greaseproof paper. Peel or scrape the carrots and grate them finely. Cream the margarine and sugar until light and fluffy. Separate the eggs and beat the yolks into the creamed mixture with the lemon juice and orange rind. Sieve the flour and baking powder together and beat lightly into the creamed mixture. Fold in the walnuts and carrots. Whisk the egg whites to stiff peaks and fold into the mixture. Put into the tin, hollowing the centre slightly with the back of a spoon. Bake for 1 hour. Cover with a double sheet of greaseproof paper and continue to cook for 30 minutes. Cool in the tin for 10 minutes and turn on to a wire rack to cool.

When the cake is cool, it may be eaten plain, but is particularly delicious with the icing. Make this by beating together the cheese, honey and lemon juice. Swirl over the top of the cake, using the back of a dessert spoon, and decorate with walnut halves.

BAVARIAN APPLE CAKE

SERVES 8
175 g (6 oz) plain flour
100 g (4 oz) vegetable margarine
3 tablespoons milk
675 g (1 ¹/₂ lb) eating apples
2 tablespoons fresh breadcrumbs
50 g (2 oz) mixed dried fruit
50 g (2 oz) light soft brown sugar
25 g (1 oz) mixed chopped candied peel

pinch of ground cinnamon
pinch of ground ginger
pinch of ground nutmeg

Preparation time: 15 minutes
Cooking time: 40 minutes
Preheat the oven to 180°C/350°F/Gas mark 4.

Grease a baking sheet. Sieve the flour into a bowl and rub in the margarine until the mixture is like fine breadcrumbs. Mix to a soft dough with the milk. Roll out to a rectangle about 30 x 20 cm (12 x 18 inches). Peel and core the apples and slice them thinly. Mix in a bowl with the breadcrumbs, dried fruit, sugar, peel and spices. Arrange down the centre of the pastry, leaving about 5 cm (2 inches) down each side. Fold this pastry over, leaving a strip of the apple mixture visible down the centre. Place on the baking sheet and bake for 40 minutes. Cool on the baking sheet and lift off carefully onto a serving dish. If liked, the cake may be iced with a little sugar mixed with lemon juice or water. This cake may be served at the end of a meal, with cream if liked.

BLACKBERRY CAKE WITH CINNAMON TOPPING

MAKES 15 PIECES
100 g (4 oz) vegetable margarine
100 g (4 oz) light soft brown sugar
1 egg
225 g (8 oz) plain flour
2 teaspoons baking powder
¹/₄ teaspoon salt
150 ml (¹/₄) pint milk
225 g (8 oz) blackberries

Topping:
100 g (4 oz) light soft brown sugar
50 g (2 oz) vegetable margarine
50 g (2 oz) plain flour
¹/₂ teaspoon ground cinnamon

Preparation time: 15 minutes
Cooking time: 1 hour
Preheat the oven to 180°C/350°F/Gas mark 4.

Grease and line the base of a 27.5 cm (11 x 7 inch) cake tin with greaseproof paper. Cream the margarine and sugar and beat in the egg. Sieve the flour with the baking powder and salt, and beat into the creamed mixture with the milk. Spread in the prepared tin.

Wash the berries and drain them very well. Sprinkle over the surface of the cake mixture. Make the topping by creaming together the margarine and sugar and working in the flour and cinnamon to make a mixture like breadcrumbs. Sprinkle evenly over the blackberries. Bake for 1 hour. Cool in the tin and cut into squares before removing. Eat freshly baked.

FRESH PLUM CAKE

MAKES ONE 17.5 CM (7 INCH) ROUND CAKE
175 g (6 oz) caster sugar
100 g (4 oz) vegetable margarine
2 eggs
1 lemon
100 g (4 oz) self-raising flour
1/2 teaspoon vanilla essence

Topping:
225 g (8 oz) ripe plums
2 tablespoons caster sugar
1 tablespoon ground almonds
1/2 teaspoon ground cinnamon

Preparation time: 15 minutes
Cooking time: 1 hour
Preheat the oven to 190°C/375°F/Gas mark 5.

Grease and line the base of a 17.5 cm (7 inch) round cake tin with greaseproof paper. Cream the sugar and margarine. Beat the eggs lightly together. Grate the lemon rind and squeeze out the juice. Sieve the flour. Add the eggs, lemon rind and the juice, flour and vanilla essence to the creamed mixture, beating well. Put into the prepared tin and bake for 15 minutes.

Meanwhile cut the plums in half and discard the stones. Mix together the sugar, ground almonds and cinnamon. Slide the cake a little way from the oven and quickly arrange the plums on top, cut side up and close together. Sprinkle with the sugar mixture. Continue baking for 45 minutes. Leave in the tin to cool. Lift carefully on to a serving plate, and serve freshly baked .

BONFIRE PARKIN

MAKES ONE 27.5 X 17.5 CM (11 X 7 INCH) CAKE
350 g (12 oz) medium oatmeal
100 g (4 oz) wholemeal flour
1 teaspoon ground ginger

100 g (4 oz) vegetable margarine
100 g (4 oz) clear honey
100 g (4 oz) black treacle
4 tablespoons milk
$^{1}/_{2}$ teaspoon bicarbonate of soda

Preparation time: 15 minutes
Cooking time: 1 $^{1}/_{2}$ hours
Preheat the oven to 160°C/325°F/Gas mark 3.

Grease and line the base of a 27.5 x 17.5 cm (11 x 7 inch) cake tin with greaseproof paper. Stir together the oatmeal, flour and ginger in a bowl until evenly coloured. Put the margarine, honey and treacle in a pan and heat gently until the margarine has just melted. Beat into the dry ingredients. Heat the milk to lukewarm and stir in the soda. Beat into the mixture and pour into the prepared tin. Bake for 1 $^{1}/_{2}$ hours. Leave in the tin for 10 minutes and then turn onto a wire rack to cool completely. Wrap in greaseproof paper and store in an airtight tin for 3 days before cutting.

This is a traditional gingerbread eaten on Bonfire Night. It is very solid and filling, and is excellent for a packed lunch or tea.

WALNUT BITES

MAKES ONE 20 CM (8 INCH) SQUARE CAKE
225 g (8 oz) light soft brown sugar
1 egg
75 g (3 oz) plain wholemeal flour
1 teaspoon bicarbonate of soda
$^{1}/_{2}$ teaspoon ground nutmeg
$^{1}/_{2}$ teaspoon salt
100 g (4 oz) chopped walnuts

Preparation time: 5 minutes
Cooking time: 20 minutes
Preheat the oven to 180°C/350°F/Gas mark 4.

Grease and line the base of a 20 cm (8 inch) square tin with greaseproof paper. Put the sugar and the egg into a bowl and beat well. Mix together the flour, soda, nutmeg, salt and walnuts, stir into the mixture until well blended. Spread in the prepared tin. Bake for 20 minutes. Cool in the tin and cut into squares before lifting out carefully. For a special occasion, spread melted chocolate on the cake, or a little icing sugar mixed with hot water and a little coffee essence.

What is the WI?

If you have enjoyed this book, the chances are that you would enjoy belonging to the largest women's organization in the country – the Women's Institutes.

We are friendly, go-ahead, like minded women, who derive enormous satisfaction from all the movement has to offer. The list is long – you can make new friends, have fun and companionship, visit new places, develop new skills, take part in community services, fight local campaigns, become a WI market producer, and play an active role in an organization which has a national voice.

The WI is the only women's organization in the country which owns an adult education establishment. At Denman College, you can take a course in anything from car maintenance to paper sculpture, from bookbinding to yoga, or cordon bleu cookery to fly-fishing.

All you need to do to join is write to us here at the **National Federation of Women's Institutes, 104 New Kings Road, London SW6 4LY**, or telephone 071 371 9300, and we will put you in touch with WIs in your immediate locality. We hope to hear from you.

About the Author

Mary Norwak has written over 100 books, including *The Farmhouse Kitchen, English Puddings* and more than a dozen titles on freezer cookery. She gives cookery demonstrations to many different groups. A member of the WI for over 30 years, Mary Norwak belongs to Cley WI and has served on the Executive Committee of the Norfolk Federation of Women's Institutes.